A Melody in My Heart

Rosemary Stankwytch Long

Cushing Publishing
www.cushingpublishing.com

I would like to dedicate this book to my family, especially my grandchildren. Thank you for your love and support.

Table of Contents:

You Are My Song

You are my prayer
You are my only place, and
I know you are there.
In You, always, let me be found.
Hold me close to Your loving heart.

How I Know That God is Real

My viewpoint is skewed – faulty
A smoky mirror without enough light
I cannot hold up an image that proves –
I know because He has told me
A created voice in me that must speak
Not caring how I am heard
      if I am understood
      if any other likes or approves
Even if no one cares
      one way or the other
I give what He gave
      back to Him
      to glorify Him
As only I can
In the ways He created me to be.
Bathed in splendor
To know and be known of God
The God of Real.

Full of Glory

How do I know God's purpose for me
I know what I must do -- what
I must do this in order to breathe.
This is how I give true praise to my creator
Flawed, imperfect that I am--
will always be in this life
Here is where my heart sings,
Overflows
Here is where my heart is full of You
Where I know you best
Where joy is absolutely unspeakable and full of glory.

Breath by Breath

There is a song from the 1971 Rock opera Godspell that played in my head all day yesterday.

> "...three things I pray.
>
> To see thee more clearly,
>
> Love thee more deary,
>
> Follow thee more nearly
>
> Day by day."

Day by day. One day at a time. Whatever this day brings. Sufficient to the day. Sometimes, Lord, that is too much time for me to handle. I need your presence – breath by breath.

I need to see you, yes.

I also need to see me through your gracious love when I am alone and afraid of the day's journey.

I need to see all of me and all of others through the lens of your forgiveness. By the blood of the lamb.

Help me to see every heart, every life, the way you do – starting with my own.

Help me to see your face in every face -

Your light waiting to shine in every dark corner -

Your grace is eager to be embraced -

Your goodness – hovering like a new mother over every hurt place.

You asked Peter three times if he loved you.

How do I love you?

I cannot fetch you a blanket or make your favorite meal.

Time at your feet? Time in prayer? Time in study? Time in service to the least of these?

It is so easy to say the words. To make the promises – resolutions if you will. Easily made, easily broken.

Prune me. Break me. Empty me.

Whatever needs doing that I may be filled with your Spirit.

Breath by breath.

Seed for Harvest

Truth is hard and flat. A tabletop.
A plateau, a stage. A firm foundation.
A level place where it is safe to run, safe to dance.
I sing a song of delight.
I sing of freedom.
I cannot explain my joy.
There are no words that truly tell my journey.
From the hills, the valleys, the depths, and the heights
Over which my faith tumbles and leaps.
I have sewn in tears.
Seed for a harvest.
Seed that yields.
Seed burned up on the road.
Seed for living and for dying.
Some for a harvest.
Seed for rejoicing.
Seed for Truth.
My God, you have delivered me!
You have done great things in me.
My life, and my heart has gotten big.
Big enough to truly know who you are.
The spirit of Truth living in me.
Knowing me.
Singing to me.
Leaping inside of me with joy that cannot be spoken.

Shelter

Carefully, I step down from a place
that once was high.
An edge crumbles beneath my foot as I cast
A backward glance
To the altar, where once
I danced.
Within me, my spirit, heavy –
like the clouds that surround me –
Still weeps for a new day along an old path
Worn smooth by many steps.
Can I find my way before the storm rages –
Or must I fight wind and wave to find the shore.
The tabernacle built on my high place
Can not shade me or give me shelter that will not fall.
Walls, worn smooth with expectation, are crumbling now.

I cannot look back like a stubborn heart
Determined to find what the Lord has removed.
My Lord said follow me—
He has left that place
I so loved and revered *because* He was with me there.
I must be where He is – where He goes –
I will be like Ruth, not like Lot's sad and broken wife.
I will not become a salt pillar marking my loss.
I will be salt scattered – flavor and blessing
Where He goes. Where He leads.

My God will be my shade –
my place of refuge –
my home and my hiding place –
A shelter from storm and rain
– the deluge will not beat me down.
The winds that roar will not strike me down.
My God will secure my dwelling –
My Abba will lift me
Cover me with glory.
His mantle is a shelter for the people –
He is a strong deliverer for us.
There is a refuge, rest, and glory
In His shadow, in His secret place –
Carved in the palm of His hand.

Isaiah 4:6
Joel 3:16

My God My Redeemer

You have put to flight everything that once threatened
me –

You have put to shame every enemy that sought to hurt –

My God, My Redeemer.

You have loved me in my disgrace, in my deepest hurt,
my darkest mind.

Embraced me while I was yet broken, and filthy. A
chipped pot.

So I was and so I am. Yet

You believe in me.

My God, My Redeemer.

Too dark to see where I am

Too deeply hurt to know what brings this pain –

You looked past my unraveled life

And took the weight of sin away.

Can I explain my fall – can I explain what stole my hope?

Can I reject the whispered threat, the silent shame, the
dangling rope?

My God, My Redeemer – I turn to you with nothing left.

Only You can heal my heart. Only you –

My God, My Redeemer.

You have put to flight everything that once threatened
me –

You have put to shame every enemy that sought to hurt –

My God, My Redeemer.

When the hour is dark, I finally call.

Forgiveness First...

Would you be free from memories
     that torment
     that just waste you
        at the drop of a word
        a name
        a place
     a moment past
but not forgotten
Would you unstrap
     that baggage
     the heavy heavy load
     for which there is no purpose
But to weigh you down
     slow you down
     pull you down
     again
Into a dark place
     a place of misery
     of regret
Would you love like Christ
In a world that does not
does not forgive
does not forget
does not even care
A world that chooses
who it favors
What is on display

strength
beauty
clever words
Would you give it all
     every bit of your life
     every gift
Give it all to a God who commands
     out of love –
     obedience –
     out of love.
Let it never be fear of God
     that commands
     or pursues me
     when I stand
     at a crossroads
     and choose –
Because I love Him
     I obey Him
Every blessing
Every good thing
Every one is mine but
Forgiveness is first.
I must forgive so I am free
     free to live
     free to love
Like Christ.

Nothing at All

Missing you greatly as I see
What lovely care you took of me
With an eye out for
      danger
      foolishness
When I was adrift
      you grabbed hold
Together we steered better.

I can't believe the utter vile
audacity of some folks
      I think it is part mental decline
      part lonely desperation.
Has my compassion turned against me?
Finally exposed for the mush pot I am –
      too eager to care
      too eager to not judge
      too uncertain
      to stand my ground
And say
Away with you! Scoundrel!
Out of my way – you devil!
There is nothing here for you.
Nothing at all.

I'm holding on to all of me
Saving it up

Until the veil parts for me
When – still in Christ –
I see my true love
My sweetheart
Again.
There is not one thing wrong with that
Nothing at all.

Served

Early morning vision – a banquet table—
A feast of celebration—
I am a server.
I serve everyone – Anyone
Highways and byways – come on in –
Faces in a crowd –
Friends and family –
Even myself.
Then I spotted you.
Waiting. Loving –
Giving me the space to come to myself
And come to you.

I see gifts on the table –
Not just the sparkling china, the flowers and crystal
The snowy white linen –
Or the wonderful food, but also sweet mementos –
Personal touches.
Kindness and goodness displayed
In the works of your hand –
In wood and pearl and finest silver –
But there is none for you.
No gift at your place.
You have not been served.

I search for something I can
Quickly construct

Fabricate from my own treasures –
What gift can I bring?
Why have you not been served?

My heart, yes – it is yours.
My love is true – I honor you because
There is no one like you –
This I know.

I hear a song –
　　"You can have all this world – Give me Jesus"
Yes. All I want. Everything I need.
Give me Jesus.
You rise quietly –
Capture my mind –
Gently touch my soul –
　　"You can keep all your treasure – I desire you. Give
me you."
You kneel before me as a servant –
Pour warm water on my tired and dusty, bruised feet –
Showing me how to be.

Inheritance

Incorruptible, undefiled
That fadeth not away---

Reserved in Heaven,
A lively hope
That none can take away.

Foolish to the world is our reward---
Untold riches, safely stored
Where thieves can not break in.

I Peter 1:4 and Matthew 6:19-20

The Word of God

Living and full of power
Sharp and to the point
Sharper than the sharpest
A two-sided knife --
Easily dividing what holds us together
And what feeds our being.
Joints and marrow.
Not so we cut each other up or
Use our sword to remove a speck
From a cloudy, tender eye
But to cut the cancer from ourselves –
To remove the selfishness and lovelessness
From our own hearts.

Good Eyes – Learning to See

Do I have them?

My optometrist would shrug, point out my advancing age.

"There is no evidence of eye disease'

He delivers this news like a Band-Aid to cover the age faux pas.

No glaucoma.

No macular degeneration.

No retinal bleeds.

No near or far in excessive amounts.

I can see to drive without my glasses,

But they stay on my face until I lay me down to sleep…

What would you say Jesus?

You are the perfect picture of good eyes.

Your compassion and mercy

Unparalleled and righteous

All witness to your good eyes.

You even see the end from the beginning

You see right through me to joints and marrow

To the condition of my heart.

Superman eyes.

Precious Lord, you who are the visible image of the invisible God –

What do others see in me, yes,

But more, what do you see?

I want a good eye. Full of grace and truth.

A reflection of your loyal faithful committed love

Trustworthy and reliable.

Keep me from bad eyes – critical angry eyes
Unkind unforgiving eyes.
Eyes that look for spots in everyone else's.
Unfettered roaming bad eyes –
Refusing to see -- ayin ra'ah—
Greedy and stuffed full of good things,
Blind to the needs of others –
Stingy – resenting those blessed with more
Clinging grasping – always wanting
Refusing to help others.
Looking for the worst and finding it
No longer recognizing favor when it comes.
Suspicious and trusting no one, Lord
Not even you –
Pure misery – It's contagious.

I will be judged as I have judged.
Help me Lord to see others with a good eye
Full of light to see the good
Eyes that expect to find it
Light and love so generous – full of good will
Rejoicing when others prosper – when they flourish
Hoping for their happy and healthy life on your good earth.
A life full of good things – like I want for me and mine.
A good eye – ayin tovah
Learning to see.

Matthew 6: 22-23; Proverbs 22: 9; Exodus 34: 6

Queen of the World

If I were Queen of the World
      or even just 'Queen for a Day'
My throne would be a pedicure chair
      full deluxe service model with all the options.
My feet would be soaked in fragrant waters –
Lounging in all the lotions,
Bubbling in the bubbles,
Flexing all my foot muscles in the fragrant air–
While emollients surrounded each little piggie
All day. Every day.

My throne would be the model that massages
      every aching place
until I am numb with happiness.
Drowning my rough heels in sweet oils –
      sluffing off the wasted skin
      making my feet new
Making my feet fit to carry good news.

How lovely, how beautiful
      even when I have traveled on rough roads
      across mountains steep
high places – rocky places.
If my message is good news of peace and salvation –
My feet are beautiful.

The young Asian woman who diligently offers

her very best care

Has no idea of the lofty, 'Royal' thoughts

running through my head

She speaks English a tiny bit and understands less.

She cannot tell me with words

to do this

or that instead

Does she see my goodwill as we bumble along together?

Perhaps she does.

Respectfully masked

I can see her eyes laugh

When I do something awkward with my feet

I smile at her patient kindness.

I pray for her happy healthy life.

I pray she hears the good news.

If I were queen of the world...

Isaiah 52:7; Romans 10:15

When I was a single young woman, whenever I was at home, I would always care for my Daddy's feet. I would sit on the floor and clip and file and rub and anoint with lotions while he spoke wisdom to me. If I could do that one more time... If I were queen of the world.

Keepers of Awe

From you, I seek comfort when my mind is troubled
by minutia, by temporal, petty things.
You Lord, comfort me with your Word whispered in my
heart;
>With the vastness of your love
>And the astounding evidence of your creative
power,
You tremble me.
So many created ones. So many people, each one unique.
>How did you do that, starting with two.
The changing panorama of the sky
>The colors of a sunset, each one vivid
>The stillness of the night sky when I stand alone
in a quiet place
And witness completely breathtaking high above me.
>So many stars, so many worlds.
>And yet, you enter into this one in such amazing
ways.
Your handiwork in all this world – beyond anything I
could imagine.
I am filled with awe at your greatness, your vastness –
And yet I know you see me
You answer every time I call
You live right here with me, beside me, in me.
When fear attempts to distract me
When concern for tomorrow pushes away my precious
today
You remind me.
I witness your mighty works – all of Creation –

the sun and the moon in their never-failing orbits

All the beauty of the Earth contained within its place by your hand

The Seasons change and even in the midst of all, you stand.

You know the ruin perpetrated by us who were called to be

Stewards – to protect and reign – to nurture and increase all the treasures

of the Earth.

Called to share all the bounty your hand has provided.

The seasons do not fail because you have commanded.

So, Spring comes and trees bud

Summer comes and they bloom in every color of life and shade the Earth

Autumn comes and the fruit of the trees covers the ground like a

coat of many colors

Winter also, and the trees stand waiting for you to speak life.

The Earth is not new

Those you created to be like you have failed to cherish your gift

of air and water and life.

We honor

We idolize only what we make ourselves out of stone and wood –

steel and concrete

promises broken

seeds scattered where they fall

faithlessness in every form.

Oh Lord, God of all we see and know

Redeemer and friend

Teach us once again to be in awe of you
And to keep awe as a holy fire burning
That will not let us forget.

Clothed

I dreamt that I gave you--
the Lord,
the creator of everything--
a coat.
It was a coat made with unskilled hands--
not with fine thread
not with soft wool
but dull in spots
torn in places--
In need of a good mending.

This coat was not beautiful to me
It was not special,
But it was what I had made.
When we give a garment,
It should be at worst, gently used,
Or at least, greatly loved, if going sad.

This coat that I gave to the One I so love
Was none of these things.
This One in whom there is all power
This One I love not just for what He does--
This One I love for all his ways and character; His
holiness, mercy and kindness.
One who is majestic, regal--
The image of Lordship.
This One that did not need my patched and ragged coat.

But you accepted it
and put it on
and it became before my eyes
the most beautiful raiment I have ever seen.
It fit you perfectly.
You smiled at me and strutted a bit
in this coat made of broken places and emptiness
and longing
and love.
Made completely of my heart's cry
and my soul's need.

My every breath became deeper and purer
as you likewise
Clothed me in yourself and
I rested in your presence.

Communion

Show us our sin –
If we can bare to look
As we ask you to ameliorate our suffering
To take our pain and heal our diseases.
We do not understand all you paid
When your body was bruised –
When you suffered every pain
The full price of the pride of Eden
The utter betrayal by your created son.
You have already done all we need.
It is finished, after all.
We take the cube of white bread
Or the torn piece of sweet bread
Or the tasteless wafer
Without seeing the body of the begotten
In tatters –tatters – skin torn
Muscles and tendons stretched unstrung.
We think to partake of your suffering
And your healing as if we are blind.

We ask from you like we would ask Grandma
For another serving of pie – sure of success –
Knowing her rules are easily bent.
You are my Savior, forgiveness is what you do –
We ask without unearthing the buried evidence
Without acknowledging our brokenness
Without reverence of the cost to you.

You who loved the earth you created
You loved your human life
And you left all for me.
Blood poured out – the final sacrifice
Upon the altar of heaven
Final forgiveness and
Forever love.
Unending unconditional amazing merciful

When we take the cup of juice or wine
Soaked in the bread or poured in a cup
Portioned in plastic
A simile for suffering –
Once again accepting what you provide
Forgiveness past present and future.
Without a glance at our personal sin
Our pride avarice lust at issue, but not
Confessed for what it is.
The facts of why you had to save me—
From the pride that says I am right and others aren't
From my wandering, from the bent towards my will
From wrong desires
The determination to chart my course
Pull on those boot straps until I
Change myself. Change others.
Cleaning up what others see on the outside
Neglecting the health of my soul and not seeing
Love laid down upon a stone
Love lifted up from the earth –
His banner over me.
I am his and he is mine –

A lamb to the slaughter
Blood poured out in a healing flood.
"Come thou fount of every blessing"

Bind my heart
Light my path
Commune with me until
I am fixed, totally undivided, upon who you are
And the debt only you could pay.

Having Done All

Every child of the Father
Receives a "Crown of Life"
Mine is not like yours
Yours is not like mine
Both are beautiful
Both will be cast before the Lamb
Well done, you pray?
How can we know
Secure that our purpose was fulfilled
Every life has one
Every purpose is part of God's plan
There is a pursuit
Where I am meant to pour my life
Everything fits together.

But what about collapse?
When things fall apart
When knots tangle
When the world ensnares.
This world where I am emersed
Where you are emersed
Where some are drowning
This fallen world is a land of captivity
Of greed and suspicion
Of chains that bind
It always has been –
It will always be.

Who will rescue me?
Who can heal my broken heart?
Who can deliver me from this prison?
Who can enable me to see, to hear, to really know
The mind of the Father –
His will for me –
His purpose.

What is the Truth? How do I know it?
Help me stand, O Lord when trouble rages like a flood.
Cover me with your righteous mercy
Save me from ruin.
Put your peace in me, around me, in front and behind
Give me faith to believe in your salvation.
For I cannot save anyone.
Not even myself.
When the earth trembles
When mountains are cast down
When life is too much
When it is not enough
Even then, **_having done all_** –
Having taken your all upon me like a suit of armor –
Help me to stand.
Help me to see.

Revival

In my vision, I walk into a small forsaken room
With many chambers on either side –
The chambers of my heart.
Places where grief and sorrow
Have cut me – caused me to bleed.
I see the crowded closet where I keep offenses – real and
imagined –
Hoarded wrongs – fears and regret –
In stacks like discarded news –
they line the walls.
I see yet another chamber
it is a throne room covered in dust.
This is the place where I first promised my heart,
Where I sang songs of love and praise.
Where we met together in sweet communion.
Where I used to fall upon my knees –
Where I worshiped you as God alone –
Where I danced with joy in your presence.
But now I find shards of glass
broken stones
splintered wood.
Evidence of idols and false worship
Lies I have told to myself in the darkness.
Things that do not last fill up what was once a holy place.
How do I make this right?
I love you
I long for revival
of my own life

of my church.

Tell me just and merciful God what you desire.

You alone are God

 you hear

 you see

 you heal

 you provide

From wrong desires

you protect me.

I will tear down

I will purge

I will throw out everything that stands unworthily –

That blocks access to your throne

The false and vile worldly loves

that keep me from knowing you –

that keep us apart.

I repent in my miserable state.

I seek to remove what stands in the way of revival,

I ask you to make straight my way back.

Testament

Today the paper said there is no peace
BUT THE SPIRIT AND THE BRIDE SAY COME!
And no more hostages will be released
BUT HE WHO HEARS SAYS COME!
Kingdoms falter; diplomacy strains
BUT HE WHO IS THIRSTY CAN COME!
And the Earth is like one with labor pains
YET, WHOSOEVER WILL, MAY COME!
The philosophies of man are tarnished brass
AND HE WHO TESTIFIES QUICKLY COMES!
And all their treasures are broken glass
EVEN SO! EVEN SO! HE COMES!

Revelation of John 22: 17 and 20

Peace, Like a River

His peace
How can I describe it
Me, the queen of anxiety –
Or at least – a faithful lady in waiting.
This indescribable peace that flows
Over every stone that blocks
Every gulf that divides.
Peace that makes me strong
Brings sweet hope for all I need.
Hope that His hand will guide and direct –
Always.
Peace that covers every hurt with healing balm.
Like a child, I embrace my Abba –
Trusting whatever He chooses for me –
Knowing He chooses well.
Then I am satisfied with good things –
Part of His beautiful plan and design.
Miraculous provision
What can I say
Your love engulfs me – the greatest gift
Closer than close friends
Like three in one – Love, Joy, Peace
Embodied together like you
Flowing gently overall.
Joy like a fountain – unspeakable
And Peace like a river –
Powerful

I submit to You
I give my life to Joy.
Everything for Love,
All of me for Peace.

Foreboding

Looking into the hidden face of the coming year,
A sense of foreboding darkens my mind.
I cannot predict the turn and shape of world events –
The nature of human struggles
Will not reset to some other time
Where I was more comfortable with the nightly news,
the workings of Congress,
the faces of strangers at Wally World.
A certain angst with a sharper edge –
A growing agitation not compatible with
Love of mankind.

If I cannot be kind,
If gentleness rules not my tongue –
What good are my declarations of love?
With all my heart, mind, and strength,
I hold to the fruits I need.
Even more, as I sense the crumbling of a society once
thought stable.

I did not fully grasp that the enemy of love
Would certainly mask as an angel of light.
If I want to have a good end (and I do), *{2 Cor 11:15]*
I need to stop fooling around with the appearance of
goodness –
Seek the true likeness of God the Father, through Christ
my Lord
And the power of the Holy Spirit.

My perspective has quietly been altered by the pile-up of
years.
I cannot reach the glory of His presence or
Emulate His character through an act of my will.
Christ shows the way of faith, the power of trusting, and
Gives me hope of a formation of character that is lasting
And authentic.

Foreboding.
 It is real – a call to prayer.
This foreboding does not evacuate the peace I have in
Christ.
I speak of Shalom, the peace that passes understanding.
This peace is not dependent on circumstances or world
events.
This peace goes deeply into the fiber of daily life.
This peace commands me to fear not,
Even when a cause for dread surrounds me and
Tribulations arise on every side.
This peace does not hide the shadows through which I
walk,
But focuses on the one who will not let me walk through
them alone.

Foreboding.
Would suck all the joy,
All of the Love others and love my neighbors.
There is no pass when my neighbor is obnoxious,
threatening, or
Opposes my values and beliefs.
Comfortable when my neighbor is either much like me, or

Safely behind borders of culture or geography.

When I send a mission group thousands of miles

But will not venture into 'that part of town'.

When my neighbor is in my face, in my space, or taking
what I think is mine –

Now, there's a rub.

I must learn the law of Love,

Speak the language of Love, and

Practice the acts of Love.

I must embrace the power of Love to change even me.

For God so loved the world.

All for love, Christ died.

All for love, He lives and calls

To follow His ways and

Become more like Him.

Now there is a resolution worthy of my time.

AMA (Against Medical Advice)

Today was just another day to some people, or most.
Today was a different day to others, some I know...... one
is me.
I choose to remember today.
Others will want to forget.

Someone died today. I know of one.
I had wandered out once again with my sore eyes
unprotected.
The cool drizzle had stopped mixing with the clouds of
yellow springtime dust on its way down.
Pollen falling as watery drops of watercolor butter.
It was not hot or windy, just yellow.

I was walking back inside the ER for the last time today.
A junky overburdened car had just pulled squarely
before the sign that reads emergency vehicles only.
Were they blind or did they not see or care?
So many in one small limping Chevy.

I was through security and one door away from patient
care.
I glimpsed through the big doors, this white car painted
yellow
opening its doors slowly.
No one seemed to be getting out very fast.
Then I was back.
They led me to a room used for talking.

Set aside from the traffic

For treatment of the other part of humanity

The part they cannot so easily address.

I was left to wait.

Waiting gets easier for me the more I do it.

Then suddenly there is a wailing, what the Irish call keening.

Other worldly sounds of loss denial grief frustration.

They explained when they came back. *Someone died today.*

And my husband made good on his threat

and left all that world-class medicine behind him.

He would have left me too, but someone reminded me of my duty.

That is what I said.

Thank you for reminding me of my duty.

Admire my nobility as I say goodbye.

A social worker was just ahead of me.

Someone sent to move the white Chevy that was empty now.

No wonder it is such a tired place.

But in that place, anyone might learn

That the ultimate set up for failure is an attempt to control death.

My man is in his yard now, watering his azaleas.

He is not feeling bad.

He is not wired up for medical miracles.

He ate his home-cooked spaghetti supper with gusto.

I told him I felt I had failed as a wife.

As if I could lengthen his life
Or stall his fall.

So I give it back.
Whatever control I thought I had is surrendered.
I will love, cherish, and wait.
I will live my own life beginning today.
Starting right now
in a different way.

My daughter, done with homework,
possessing a legal license to drive... watching tv.
Get up.
Get dressed.
Go meet your boyfriend at the mall.
Have a ball.

Remember someone has to stay up until you come home.
Are you serious? You don't care?
I care. I will be here when you return.
It was the right thing to do.
To hell with advice.

Regret

Wasted time spent on greedy
Self-focused on regret--
It never changed a thing
Never changed a heart
Can not replace the loss
Can not wipe my tears
Or end my suffering.
The things I did not say when
the day was open wide
Tender spent emotions
left outside to die.
It will not regain the
effort unmade and yet --
Even when I can't remember,
It won't let me forget.
A cure gently spoken
binds up my broken heart --
Teaching me to love my enemies,
making friends out of memories
And joy out of regret.

I would not give up what I have learned
To get back what I have lost.

Grinding

This is hard – this is grinding.

This is a new thing.

Motherhood –was a new thing too but

I figured out the mechanics quick enough

How to fit a cloth diaper

So that little bottoms do not leak

And spoil the precious moment –

How to get the nipple into a tiny mouth

How to clothe so that little bodies are not pinched

How to coax sleep

How to cool a fever

How to breathe deep when every reflex struggles toward
fear

How to trust and let go

How to let them leave.

Motherhood is hard.

Becoming an orphan (at any age)

Losing a job

Losing a home

Betrayals – the thorns surrounding the rose that smelled
so sweet.

Friends who gladly receive but have nothing to give.

Losing my religion –

Finding the love of God in the worst moment

And the darkest place.

All of that is hard.

But this is grinding.

I cannot imagine relief.
If it comes, I will be amazed.
A new thing to learn.
I never did like the pack so alone is not so bad
In my rear view, it works for me
But this is grinding.

God is Not a Formula

He GETS Math –
He really does
He even LOVES Math –
He created it.
That does not mean He wants to BE Math.
God is not a formula.
God is not an 'ALSO' Ran.
God does not ever claim second.
Even when it is offered lovingly by our
almost perfect hand.
God is ALL even if you are nothing.
God is not an 'Also' Ran.

God is not a Fair-Weather Friend.
When everything is coming on wonderful
And I am fairly pleased
with my personal outcome
I can find many friends.
Good Friends.
Some Better.
Par-Tay.

But this I know.
If I come to the end of myself and I have alienated
Every other possibility
And I look around for just one friend
I know who it will BE.

He always IS.

He will call my name and I will know His voice.

God is not a Memory.

Your Sons and Your Daughters

They are not you.
Not an extension of you.
Not clones, not copies – each is unique.
Fearfully and wonderfully made
God's creation
not yours.
Each is responsible to Him for the choices they make
not you.
Created for His purposes and His glory
not yours.
You are not their judge.
You cannot reward nor punish eternally.
Life will teach them more than you.
The giver of life will lead them
In the way that He led you.
The lover of their soul will woo them
Just like He wooed you.

Much Speaking

Our Much Speaking
Our clever phrase
Our potent simile
Our pious posture
Our tired but true –
Trite – before the Almighty!
Many words cannot fill an empty heart
Or give joy where there is none.
Or stir up faith that can stand the test.
Or comfort, or bless, or restore, or heal or redeem.
Logos, Living Word, speak to me and through me
I need to hear you
The world needs to hear you.
Much Speaking is not helping.
Let my heart's cry be my prayer
As I touch you, as you know me.

"And when you pray, do not use meaningless repetition as the Gentiles do,
for they think they will be heard because of their many words." Mathew 6:7

Tell Me You Love Me

Tell me you love me when you lay down to sleep
Greet me each morning with joy
Show me you trust me when you kneel to pray –
Tell me your burning desire.

I love to listen to the sound of your voice
All I want is to be by your side
In the hour of temptation and season of need
Tell me your burning desire.

Close your eyes and speak my name
I am the lover of your soul
Bring every burden and question to me
Tell me your burning desire.

Quiet Rest

I shudder – I actually tremble
I'm thinking this is a flashback
I'm living through it again
I've lived through it before
My God, surround me
Cover me up, shelter me with might and power
Place me in the shadow of your wings, that I might live.

The invader – that sly devil –
Would take my house
Would break my house
Trample my vineyards and end my life before my days are
full.
But I trust in You, Jehovah –
the God who covers me
the God who delivers me
the God who takes recompense
From those who sneak and steal and lie.
Vengeance is yours.
Judgement is yours.

O righteous God of mercy and grace –
Do not reward my life with the fruit of my wandering
But renew me with the fruit of your Holy Spirit
Refresh my dry bones with your life.
Give me peace again –
Take away my trouble

Rescue my house and all who live in it.

Make us bondservants to your name

Destined to speak your word and restore the blessings of our ancestors.

That great crowd of witnesses before the throne.

Remove the stench of death that lingers and

Replace darkness with pure light.

Shine upon the path You give me –

the way You choose for all my house.

Flood me with goodness, so everyone will see the God I serve.

Open my mouth and fill it with wisdom –

do not let foolish worthless words be spoken –

Tie my tongue in a knot until You expand my joy

And fill me with praise.

Let me inhale the sweet savor of your Holy Presence all my days.

I weep with gladness – relief shakes me

I am awake – I am alive

I am happiest in your footsteps.

Happiest alone with you in quiet rest.

Isaiah 66:5

(There is a place of quiet rest, near to the heart of God –
a place where sin cannot be molested, near to the heart of God.....)

Search for Approval

Life lived in search of approval
From anyone –
Waiting for a pat on the back
Measuring success by letters after your name
Human approval
      even from love
Cannot produce true joy

Seek the approval of God.
Please Him first.
Love Him, draw close.
Get to know Him
Spend some time.
You cannot know someone
To whom you are a stranger.

Advancing

Here I sit where
Much has changed
Never the same
Some ways good
Others not
But I am what I am
I've got what I've got
I miss where I sat
Pursuing my prize
But I am who I am
Taking the hill
Not all I once was
But moving still

To the Woman on South Saunders Street

Every day I see you
Every day the same
Your face is now familiar
But I do not know your name
In piles of cluttered memory
Beside the busy street
You watch me as I pass you
But our blue eyes never meet.
Every day I leave you
Still lonely, still afraid
Reaping every consequence
Of choices poorly made.
With rapid steps, I leave you
To loneliness and fear
Not stopping to encourage
Pretending not to hear.

Mums

Every summer – hot dry days –
I nurture and protect these –
Because I love them –
Because she first planted –
Leftovers from a landscaping long completed.
Only leftovers – just a few, not an abundance.
Every year, I propagate new plants.
Easily done. They break.
I take the broken piece and with
New dirt, the sun, and the rain come –
New plants to share, to increase.
She also planted in me, in my heart.
With love, with abundance.
In the autumn of time
These shine brightly.
New hope
Joy I cannot express any other way.

Stopping for Directions

No one does these days
Neither sage nor teen
Boy nor girl
Man nor child
No need.
GPS is everything
Except for old guys still
Gathered around a wood stove
In a far-flung corner on the way to nowhere in particular
Old guys who can tell you all about that bridge
Just down the road
How much of a load
And what to avoid.
No more use for that old map
Stuffed in the glove
Coming apart along the crease
Throw out that stubby pencil used to draw
A wobbly line between home
And where you're headed
The one with the brick-hard eraser
From too many hot days in the box.
Time was and not that long ago
When the ability to read a map
That was everything too.
Is time coming – you want to bet?
We'll punch in the coordinates
And we won't even have to drive.

A whole new world around
Falling asleep at the wheel
Driving while stupid
Accident liability.
No more driver's ed for the kiddos
No more friends don't let friends.
Life is like a journey
A road trip
Destination clearly noted
The last mile of the way
Coming coming here.
Don't mind me – I'm just sleeping.
Wake me up when I get there.

"What I Know"

"What I Know" is
How to bake cookies, cake, bread, even pie
Make roast beef,
do the perfect chicken,
soups and stew
Menus heavy with Southern charm--
Sometimes, gourmet is how I roll --
A dozen ways to Summer Squash
Even more to Sweet Potato Casserole.
How to mend. How to dye
How to tell the naked truth –
How to almost lie
To soothe an aching heart
to calm a worried mind.
How to baste –
How to paste
How to wait –
How to shut up
And keep all my knowledge to myself—
Even to the point of allowing
A screw-up in the kitchen
A dropped stitch
An untimely do-over
An appointed time just missed.
I've lived.
I've loved.
I've learned.

Go for it.

Because I know **HOW** I learned "What I Know"

Safely Home

Sometimes I feel like an empty place
And the only thing filling me
Instead of your grace
Is sadness and grief.
Loss shakes me but cannot break me
Because I have a firm foundation,
A well-lit path, a sure and steady craft
That crests these waves
And delivers me to a safe harbor.
Where you lead
I will follow
I trust you
I know who you are
Countless times, in countless ways
You have let me see
You are my champion when the world shakes
You lead me to a high secure place
A place of solace, of protection
Under your feathers
In the shadow of love's wings
I go to the rock.
You are in your holy temple.
Father, Advocate, Deliverer, El Shaddai
With you I find rest.
Lead me safely home, Father.
Safely home.

A father to the fatherless, a defender of widows,
 Is God in his holy dwelling.
God sets the lonely in families,
 He leads out the prisoners with singing;
 But the rebellious live in a sun-scorched land.
Psalm 68: 5-6

The XYZ's of Balancing

Equations must balance!
My days, my life also, but
I am not a simple equation –
Variables seem the only constant for me
There is little I sometimes control.
Life is full of unexpected reactants –
(my emotions tell me lies)
Ever changing pressure
(how must I respond)
Changing temperatures
(where am I on the pride scale)
How can I obtain
(much less maintain)
Equilibrium?
Constancy in an ever-changing storm
Where waves roll and churn
And the winds won't stop.

For my equation to balance –
Everything must be constant – in control.
And I can't control much –
The attempt at least slows down my reaction.
Open my mind and heart to Your
Patience – goodness – kindness – self-control.
I seek True North – the one constant value – the
One who never changes.

Fear

Fear does not come from the heart of God.
Fear is a spirit-
an emotional weapon to destroy our peace.
God gives unspeakable peace,
beyond understanding.
Whatever reason fear comes
It hits hard as if it can take us down with
Worry, anxiety, a broken mind.
It races as if it can overcome us
But it is all smoke and mirrors.
What should I fear when I know His love?
When He gives me everything from His omnipotent hand?

I hold in my heart everything He promised.
Why would I fear when my enemy is already beaten
broken
cast out forever
My Lord has broken the enemy's back with His bruised
heel.
Great power with no fear is mine.
Only love can heal.

Love brings peace and a sound mind.
Solid
Real

II Timothy 1:7 For God has not given us a spirit of fear, but power and love and a sound mind.

The Man of God

I will run and fetch him, and he will pray for us.
But he has stepped away too far –
too completely for me to take his hand.
I will recall his words and say them
he will hear and come.
But no, they were not his words.
Not the servant's words.
They were the words of his master, his God.

I will run
I will seek God and His place.
There, I will pray for myself
for all of us.
His place is not too far –
He is always near.
We are in Christ, who is in us.
In Him, we have peace and joy.
The veil is thin.

Come, let us all be together in Christ, forever and ever.
Amen.

Love Wins

The fires that rage around me
And beside me, within me sometimes,
They will not consume me.
No matter how hot it gets
No matter how I long for cool water,
I will not be reduced to ash.
I will pass through many troubles.
I wander through a wilderness of trouble...
But my God overcomes all;
And He keeps me always.
My God is with me
Troubles will not drown me--
Trouble cannot drown love--
Love drowns trouble.
Love wins.

Isaiah 43:2

Any Moment

You give me someone to talk to
Someone to believe
I can tell you anything
My hurts and my heart's desire

Any moment you are with me
Never alone
Loving me tenderly
Always on time

And all he asks of me is to hope for his return
As a bride does when her groom is on his way.
And always love each other
Like we do our eldest brother
To keep oil and to watch and work and pray
And on that final day,
Begin a brand-new life with you.

Any moment, we could hear him
Above the city streets or by the waters still
Our beloved surely comes
And we, his one true love
Will never hurt again.

Truth About Me

You speak to me
What I did not know.
You speak words to me
None other would know.
You are my Good Shepherd
And I know your voice.
Another will not get what I get
I might not get the same again –
What I've already had may be gone.
There is a season
a reason
Your will and your way.
Your Time for sure!
An appointed time
A place in line
Your grace forgives my slips and my trips.
Truth is in your word to me
And I trust You.
I must listen for your voice.
If I would hear.

Cover Me With Mercy

My skin testifies to injuries long healed
Sun damage – weight gained and lost –
The vestiges of Motherhood
The spot on my face fading –
How mean that I lose that sweet spot
And keep stretch marks.

My skin tone conjures preference, privilege in my world
A world at war with Your statutes
My skin covers and protects
Thinner over my bones
Thicker over my heart
Pierce my tough hide
Uncover a heart of tenderness.
Worth the wear. Worth the tear.
Jehovah Rapha – instill goodness and gentleness
In my mind, my body.
You made coats of skin in the Garden
When we were ashamed.
The skins of animals as a covering – a testimony to
mercy.
Skin taken from Abram as a covenant sign
The promise of a faithful God to Abraham.
Down from Sinai, Moses' skin shone too brightly
And we could not look upon his face.
Then law after law – So many laws
A sign of unclean
Boils and raw flesh; Hot burning skin

Death dark; Sick white
Straining knots – Choking hope
Skins on the altar
Covering what has touched the world –
Covering our brokenness.
Job was covered by bones and sinew
Skin and flesh – skin in the game
Skin for skin
All that a man has for his life
Even his skin for what is covered by skin.
Skin flayed from the body of Christ – a testimony to mercy.
The skin of my teeth, struggling to trust
More than skin-deep
Skin cleaving to my bones
Holding me together like a girdle.
They take my skin and break my bones
But You cover me with mercy.

Micah 3:3; 6:8

Put on Faces

Now, it's the time of year when children put on masks
And they pretend to be what they could never be.

Christians put on faces and think that we can hide
Anywhere but in the rock and still become His bride.

We see the fault in others – we gossip, lie, and brag
And we pretend to save ourselves by dressing up in rags.

And still, we put on faces we want the world to see
Forgetting that where treasure hides the heart will surely
be.

We know there is a season, and a time for labor pains
Jesus knows – He sees it all – He will come again.

If there is oil, it's time to buy it and clothe ourselves in
Him
For only love can wash away the crimson stain within.

It's the time of year when children put on masks
And they pretend to be what they could never be.

Not Man Made

Lord, in Psalm 61,
you tell me that one characteristic of the anointing,
one of my many blessings—
Is that along with Your favor
comes the 'day of the LORD's anger against my enemies.'
O, help me see,
to understand,
and not forget,
that my enemies are spiritual beings
not human ones.

Loving Father,
you've told me before that even though
some person thinks I am their enemy
does not mean they are mine.
Help me fully know
that people are not each other's enemies.
And that the weapons we are given
to wage war against 'enemies' and wickedness in 'high places'
are not man-made.

Boundary

A moon bright shore and the ocean is still.
But the waves are coming.
Wave after wave steadily,
Rocks become sand cast upon a distant shore.
But always within the boundary of the sea.
Sands are not cast upon the high hills far away.
The waves do not fail.
And yet, they cannot prevail.
They cannot break the boundaries set for them.

I wake from a dream and see that I am unharmed.
My children are with me, and they are free.
The enemy that coiled and struck over and over until
I fell upon my bed and only raised one arm to push it
back,
This evil thing has pulled away.
The morning sun has chased the darkness.
Evil flung its lustrous amber dark around me
But could not break the boundary set by love.

My God has set a boundary around me.
The enemy comes and comes but cannot win.
God protects; He watches forever.
Though troubles come like waves,
My God is with me, and I am not afraid.
When the way is hard, He gently eases
With the fullness of his great eternal love.
He comforts me with good things

He anoints me forever.
I stand in awe of His goodness and
I rest myself in this place
Now and forever safe.

Choose Mercy

Let mercy fall on my heart my life my family
Not as a gentle mist
But a soaking, quenching rain
That comes freely at the moment I would
Pay anything
Renounce anything
Forgive anyone
That I might stand with face up turned to receive
More than enough to fulfill my every need.

Cleanse me all the way down to who I really am
Soak down deep to the roots of my being
Choose mercy and do not let my heart grow hard.
Soften the bonds of sin so that I may be released –
As the rain soaks into the hard dry soil and softens the
drying roots
And restores what has been stolen.

What You prepared for Yourself
That You would be glorified—
Let mercy be my portion –
That You would be glorified by the fruit You nurture in
me.

Break Me

A 'good for the soul' season is coming.
I see the light shifting before me--
A time to really see
If I only will.
A time to repent
A time to confess
A time to be renewed
No stones thrown.
A time for the hidden to be revealed.
My soul cries, "Yes, Lord!"
Heal me and restore me now.
So that I will not come out of the wilderness of this world
Halt, or crippled, or lame--
But filled with joy
With a voice lifted in praise and perfect love.
Fully washed--
Absolutely clean--
I will worship you.
Break me.

Glory

Stripped bare of all my pretense
And attempts to hide the leaven –
Unveiled, I stand before you –
The King of all Creation
Lord of all the hosts of heaven.

I see you risen, glorified.
Dividing forever my heart mind and emotions –
You, the living Word
Putting asunder Everything.
So that love is on one side
And fear is sealed off on the other.

By this, I have been freed from death, hell, and the grave.
You are my portion
Today – while I live in this body.
And that precious day when I first saw your glory,
And now forever more – from glory to glory
Being remade in your image.

Removing my splintered mask
Clearing my clouded eye
Cleansing my wicked
Desperately broken heart
Bringing new life – glory to glory.

Increase in me

Become more – greater and more real
Until I see –
In that first glimpse of eternity –
All of your beauty and love
All of your glory.

Good News

I embrace good news in a world short on good
Long on bad
Full of evil.
I run to the rock.
Under the shelter of His Love – a hiding place
Lovely and secure.
Through a glass darkly – scratched lenses
Perhaps a new RX is needed.
So much fuzzy blurry clutter on my landscape
When all I want to see is Jesus –
 To see Him in all of His glory.
Faith, Hope, and Love – pure worship
A wayside place where I may rest
Be refreshed
Until I reach my Father's house
Where my salvation and all He has promised me
Is safe and secure.

He is God

God is who he says he is.
Worthy of trust—
All that he asks is that we believe that he exists
And trust he will keep his word.
He is not one of us in that he would lie.
He is truth and light and so brightly does he shine
That we could not even bear to see his face.
When I ask him to help me,
So often what I mean is for him to please give me what I
need to take over –
So that I can provide for myself, be sufficient without
him.
When all he wants is for me to trust him to meet me
wherever I am
And for him to be my God.
On the mountain top
And in the valley.
In the impossible –
In the moment when I am lost and afraid—
In the everyday mundane nothing special –
Always and forever
He is my God and I trust him.

Hidden Things

Once again, Lord.
Once again,
You ask that I search my heart
For anything I would hide from You.
How would I cover my nakedness?
What would I hide from our communion?
I see a desire for acclaim, for praise
for acknowledgment from the world.
From you, and You alone, I should seek well done.
"Well done, good and faithful" from the heart of God –
This will give quiet rest.
Yet, a secret sin troubles me,
My place where I raise an altar to another.
a high place for myself
for my own favor.
It always comes back to pride – every single time –
Forgive me Lord. Again.
I put on a mask of righteousness
But I continue to sin.
I continue to favor me.
Clean out my dark spaces –
again, Lord –
Help me give all glory to You.
Uncover my pride.
Open me in all Your ways,
So I can see the face of my pride
Then, let me hide beneath Your wings –

Draw me close and speak Your words
Until I know pure love, quiet rest,
In all the hidden things.

"There is a place of quiet rest, Near to the heart of God"

Stubborn Ears

I have stubborn ears
They itch
They have fits to hear only what they want to hear.
My eyes are stubborn too and only want to see
What they expect to see.
What exactly do I see?
Really see.
Do I need to be told what I see –
Do I want to be told what I see –
What is true?
The truth makes us free.
The truth is light.
Why do we not listen?
Why do we fight?

If I Believe

I sit here surrounded
Listening to glorious praise –
an offering beautiful and pure.
"You keep on getting' better..."
Yes, you do, but this is just too much.
It is so heavy.
I am here in this wilderness feeling lost
I am not saying mine is more –
worse than what is common.
I am just saying it is too much for me.
I am weak
I am cold and I am afraid.
It is all too much.
Too heavy for my little faith.
I hear your voice and I know
You are picking me up
Lifting me out of this pit
You rescue me from the evil that pursues me.
Every time.

"You are not meant to carry this;
You were never meant to go alone into this valley –
I will carry you
Your burdens are mine."

If I believe. Nothing is too small
        Or insignificant –

Nothing too big, too heavy, too dark, too much –
If I believe.
You are faithful – help me be like you.

Judgement

Judgement is coming
Not just to those
we think deserve it.
It comes first to those
who think they have moved past it.
It is coming to my life and yours.
It is coming to my religion and to yours.
It is coming to a nation that has the audacity to call out
We are special.
We are different.
We are Christian.
I think we are not.

Love for the Created

I hear the raucous cry of the many
Carried away by lust by greed
I hear the weeping heart of God the Father
He sent His word
Incarnate
Living with us
Aware of every need.

I see reports of death
Disease
Hearts of stone
Eaten up by pride
by hate
I see the beseeching love of Christ my King
For those who have not come –
He mercifully waits.

The bitterness of hearts
Sour words
Can't you almost taste them?

Yet the sweetness of God
The oil of joy in His presence
His salvation seasons my life
And I am free.

When I cry out for grace

His hand is open to me
I praise His glory
heaven coming down for me
I fall on my face
His mercy holds my place.

A place for me made
imagined
planned
From the dawn of the first day
Handed down from the glorious throne of the
Uncreated one
To a created one like me.

State of Being

Of the Church.
The Elect Lady.
Triumphant, spotless
The bride of Christ,
Adorned in His glorious love.
How did we ever get to this place?
Worry and striving
Losing vision
Losing faith and hope
Forgetting love.
The enemy comes to kill
To steal
To destroy
To make a way for spots and blemishes
Even so, we are redeemed by love.
Purchased
Ordained
Hope restored for the Glory of God
And for His kingdom to come
On earth as it is in heaven.
Faith found
Love, again, the first fruit among us
Ripe with longing
The way we show His glory
Proof of who we are.

My Sin

My sin – a burden you seek to remove
You willingly take it all
You did nothing to deserve my punishment
You took it all for love.
My sin – I am like everyone
My burden is significant
What you picked up was heavy and restricting
Clipping my wings
Stealing my joy
Cutting deep with no relief, but You said,
'Learn of me for my burden is light.'
Once again, you are right.

Obedience

One word sums it all
Better than perfection
Like I ever could do that –
Better than sacrifice
Of anything, you understand
Even everything I have
All I think I am.
So much more than all
Knowledge, Wisdom, even Faith
Obedience.
True love and worship.

Obedience.
Better than do or think or ask
Better to will to do His will
Seek His way
Follow His command
Always, and
In each moment
Seeking, hearing.
Obedience.

John 7:17

ReRun

Oh yeah.
I've felt this before.
Seen it acted out
      By changelings
      Amateurs
      Pros long-standing.
Too much
Too fast
I'm wary
(a polite
more acceptable way
to say I am afraid)
I trust God
But I don't trust me.
Take my hand
      gently lead
Please Lord –
      drag me if need
Be – Away from
      the crumbling edge
Safely distanced
      from the breaking fall.

But if I must walk this
      narrow height
      in order to see
      to learn to die

finally
or at least
to die again
To come under the laser
to reveal a perfect facet
of the beautiful gem
you are making of me.
Then, maybe that's ok
Maybe
I would not have it
any
other
way.

Thanksgiving for My Friend

When I am saying "Thanks" to Him
For the good things He has done,
When I rise above the problems
And remember that the Son
Is guiding, teaching, forming
Me, a vessel, a good pot, a strong cup
To fill and use, to even overflow –
And the goodness of my Lord
Swells so great inside –
That I feel I could see Heaven
Or hear angels
Or put on glory like a garment –
When He is just as real to me
As the blessings that He brings –
I remember you, I see something new;
And I know I'm really loving Jesus
When I am loving you.

That One

God loves the wayward me
    the stubborn one
    who thinks and questions
    even doubts
The one who stumbles
The one whose temper
    is a little too quick
    whose mouth is loud
    whose tongue is loose
The one who speaks from pride of life
That one.
There is power in the name of Jesus to heal that one too.

When All I Have is You...

My love has departed –
    my parents too
No siblings to all –
    so I call on you.
I'm still cooking for two
    (and sometimes four)
If only that meant
    I'm not alone anymore –
Still making quarts of soup
    in my largest pot
It will last me (no doubt)
    until the weather gets hot.
My besties are far away
    my children are too –
All I know – and all I can do –
    is wait –
When all I have is you....

My pastor died too
    and it made me so blue –
At least I don't see red __
    I don't blame you –
When sorrow comes
    in crashing waves
I know you are my shelter –
    my safe resting place.
I want to understand –

to feel that guiding hand
To know and believe
      obey the command
To know that I know and
      truly believe
When all I have is you –
I have everything I need.

Truly Known

If I truly know Abba Father,
Jesus my Lord –
I will listen – I will receive –
I will be filled with faith when He speaks.
His words are always true – always just –
A mighty sword with a razor edge –
Easily separating bones from marrow –
What I profess from who I am.

Is it possible to imitate Christ –
To do good, to love mercy, even walk humbly,
Giving all glory and honor –
Without listening
receiving
responding
faithfully to His words?
And not become sounding brass and a tinkling cymbal
Making a loud sound empty of harmony –
Empty of love.
Bringing confusion instead of peace.
Is it possible to fill that empty space
Without obedience
without worship
 without love?

But I have a safe shelter, strong and secure
Safe beneath His wings

Safe within His heart
Truly known
Secure forever in His forever love.

We the People

What happens to a society that sacrifices
Their little ones, their babies
No one would do that you say?
The Canaanites
Baal worshipers
The Vikings, the Phoenicians
The Aztecs and the Incas
On and on...
Well okay, but what **thinking** people would do such a
thing!
Ancient Greece
Ancient Rome
Ancient East,
Even Ancient Israel
Not anymore? Uganda, still.
Strange superstition
Leaving babies outside to die when they are not 'normal'
Mutilation of the outside
Removal of body parts ---
Or just blow them away
Guns blazing
Ripping into shreds the insides of little bodies
What kind of people would ever standstill
Grow numb
Move on from such a horror?
We the People.

Welcomed at the Gates

How will I, when will I learn?
Must I suffer to learn
Must I lose my place to find it?
If I am willing, obedient –
Will I have only the good things of the land?
Obedient in faith, by faith, to faith – to death.
Physical – this mortal flesh only –
Emotional – laying it all down to Eternal.
Spiritual – born fresh and clean.
Obeying as a child but no longer ignorant
          no longer chasing ungodly things
          no longer wallowing in the dirt.
But understanding Holy
Pursuing it.
When I am distressed in these hard days
Will I turn
From the dark places still fighting for a place in me?
Will I obey –
for healing
for freedom
for authority –
God delights in obedience.
More than my work,
my plans
my sacrifice
my riches scattered.
How foolish for *created in His image*

To obey any other.
I will not obey the voice of man –
The pull of religion
It's easy rules.
Nor the soft, alluring voice of all I've ever known –
I will wait and listen for more.

We become a slave when we obey.
Better to become a bondservant to the One who is Holy –
Just, righteous, merciful, and kind.
Sincerely seeking –
fearing God –
unseen and pure.
The Holy One who will someday take vengeance –
Who will make all things right and just?
Obey His voice.
Seek His wonderful will to do it.
Obey from the heart the One
Who comes to heal –
heart, mind, and body –
And deliver us all from
Destruction of every kind.
Hear the word of God
and so, confirm our faith.
By obedience and waiting
We will see the City of God coming down
And be welcomed at the gates.

I Will Still Be Me

Sometimes
Some days
This moment –
I want to run to you
Throw myself upon your altar
into your arms
With all that I have
all that I am not.
So, the dross that is my sin –
      my loss—
Is burned away
Consumed by your holiness.
When I stand pure in your holy light
I will still be me
Unafraid
At home, at peace
Forever.

When Will I Remember

Daily
every time
relentlessly--
That Your way is perfect
And my way is not.
What a load of trouble
So many hard places
Mean faces –
struggles far beyond me

Without giving You a place
Without giving You a
chance to light my path
To show me how when who where –
even the elusive why...
Desperately in search of a way out –
in - over... an alternate - a detour
Without asking the Way Maker to give me direction
Leaning the wrong way
Depending on my faulty perceptions
My limited wisdom
When all knowing
Ever present
Truly faithful waits patiently
With a candle, a torch, a burning lamp
The brilliance of the sun
Waiting,

wanting to be invited,
to be acknowledged in all Your beauty and light
So you can heal me completely
Strengthen my bones
And make the way straight.

In the Margins

Faithful in the margins
When things get dicey
When things get pricey
When shadows lurk and
Dark clouds churn my way.
What do I say when darkness falls
When it seems I've lost the path.
Love needs action
Trust needs proof
Sorry needs change

Thank You for Today

Let it be a day that draws me closer to you.
I want every breath to draw me closer.
For too long
I stumbled
For too long
I ran away
Convinced I was smart enough
courageous enough
To handle everything my way.
Even so, you loved me
You protected me
You watched every day for me.

I can see why you hate pride –
It is the one thing that pursues
like a hound of hell
Driving a stake into every living soul
Putting us off from love
Binding what was free
Stealing your goodness
Killing our joy.
Give me your strength Lord
Stand with me –
stand beside
within me
Help me reject pride
Help me see it coming

So I can kill it before it grows

Recognize before it surprises

Before it wraps even one lie around me.

Keep me gentle and meek

My life is found completely in you.

Because you are enough.

Personal Prayers

All I Need

I am not ok today
My burden feels too much
My loss, too great
I turn to you, Lord
The only one I know
      will help
      will listen
      will comfort
      will let me try and fail
      over and over again
And still love and never leave
Closer than the brother I do not have
Closer than anyone on earth could ever be.
You are everything – all I need.

Blessed am I When I Need Christ

Blessed and happy when I cry
Help me, Lord!
Filled to overflow with good things
because you are here.
Jesus, lover of my soul,
Help me to see you as you really are
So that you may be revealed in me.
In all my words,
In every look on my face,
Be so obvious
so full of your love
hidden in me
That I cannot be seen or heard without it.

Personal Prayers
Revelation 3:17-19
Colossians 1:27 "...which is **Christ in you***, the* **hope of glory***."*

My Prayer Today

That I might be like Christ
What a thought!
What desire moves my soul
To be like the perfect one
To respond to even one broken heart
      with the love
        the compassionate wisdom
That will heal and renew
Knit together along
      the cracks
      the creases
      the places where we all fold over
Hoping to protect our soft under-self
Bringing light into a dark shadowed place
Erasing pain and loss
With hope for all things new
With joy that cannot be contained –
Well, here's practice –
I'll start with me.

Fast and Slow

I had to slow down for you
As the years went down
    so did you
Your long, confident up and going
Up and left you.
While I moved the same
Always too fast for my feet
You remember –
Fast and crash
Ramblin Rosie

You slowed for me in years long gone
Trying to keep me to hold me
As you slowed for me
Waited for me.
Picking me up.
I fell a lot – still do
Up and down stairs
Walking without care
Tying my feet
Tripping on air
Seldom hurt – skinned knee
Broken toe – carrying the electric roaster
Full of Christmas ham.
Ham went flying
    and so did I.
Falling forward

Falling back
Hitting my head
Rolling like bread
Bouncing back like dough.

Then you began to fall
     to break
     break in pieces
     to move real slow.
Comparatively speaking to what you were
While I stayed steady at fast and crash –
Unless I walked with you
Then slow me down as we walk together
Support and cherish
Until we parted.

You took a new path
Walked with new feet
     long beautiful feet
     with slender tender toes.
I'm still on *this* walk
Still stumbling even falling
No one to pick me up
     Laugh as I bounce
Or slow me down
When I rush unseeing
Unsteady and weeping
From the inside out.
Fast to stop.
Slow to go.

"All night
All day
Angels watching over me,
My Lord...
All night
All day
Angels watching over me."

Enough

The drop that spilled the cup
Was not gently poured,
– just in case that thought occurred –
'Twas a total splashdown
Like an Apollo space capsule
Landing in a pond.

The gnat the camel strained at
The knot that threw the horse
The tiny little bearing hat
That turned the train off course

The final ending waited for
The truce no one could keep
The day that started with a song
That kept us all from sleep.

Enough can make its wishes known
Can scream without a word
And after years of silent ok –
Oh well –
Make no mistake
It will be heard.

First Light

When first I saw
First sensed
Your light tugging on my childish heart
I knew you claimed me then
Forgave me then
From the first, you knew my journey
You saw my weakness
knew what sin would pursue me
Before I let it toss me before it hurt

I remember that first light shining
Into my fear, my regret, my anxiety
Because they were already there
We live, we pray, we repent on a linear clock
A clock that needs to be wound
A clock that continually spins around and around
Until it winds down.

You with no beginning, no ending
You answer with eternity
        Unending mercy
Unending love
You see everything I need before I need it
Because you are the light

I struggle to find words
To praise you

To acknowledge your greatness, your goodness.
I repent over my life – beginning to ending
I have fallen and found grace to heal
I hope to learn to be like you
To imitate your great and giving heart.

Each time I fall, you are there
Just like the first time
When this sleeper woke to first light
The bright light of truth chasing the darkness
My eyes were opened to the beauty of you
And my heart knew

The bright light of truth, your truth
Unchanging, poured upon my sorrows
Upon my pain
A healing balm, restoring my soul
Bringing perfect peace from above
Igniting joy in the presence of love.

"...that the Messiah would suffer and, as the first to rise from the dead, would bring the message of light to his own people and to the Gentiles." **Acts 26:23**

A Different Season

I'm ready for a change of season – more light
A new season –
This one is used up and worn out.
Feeling left on the precipice is tiring.
Teetering on the edge gets old.

Grief does indeed come in waves.
And sometimes, like now,
I am drowning.

The spring breezes I have waited and longed for
Demonstrate their ability to turn cold –
To disappoint and delay once again.

Freezing has not kept back the evidence of fire ants
Buried deep all along my borders.
But I press on...

I will pull up every weed,
Every single one
Widow's weeds I'll call them –
Evidence of the state of my garden –
And for a time, my life.
I will clean up what is left of winter's touch
I will keep on until I see the roses blooming.
As The Rose of Sharon blooms in me again.

When winter blows across the yard
And all the seeds are asleep
When it's cold down to my bones –
To my roots –
My God is near.
For such a time, He whispers –
A sacred time –
A time to realize
What I am living through hurts you, Lord.
You cried at the tomb of Lazarus on the precipice of a
miracle –
On the cusp of spring breezes.
On the edge of coming back
Waking up
Putting out new growth.

A new season – full of light and
Clear blue skies.

To My Mother

On the Death of Her Own

Where has my other self gone
I looked – but waited too long
With no clue except that constant woe
The proclamation word from Daddy that I
Am more like you than I know.

For a long time
I saw no help in that.
Consumed with finding
All the things about you
I would change if only
Never stopping
Not seeing
That if I could
If I did
You would not be you.

Maybe now I understand
That the living, morphing you
That nursed and nurtured
Coaxed and guided
Demanded and pleaded
Lost and won –
Gave me a canvas
Upon which to draw myself

An image of me
Somehow locked inside.

A different sort of strength
A different knowledge of
What I have the power to become.
A part of you inside of me.

There was a flow between you
Your mother
Me
Now broken
A stream separated from its source.
Sharper for you.
You are now what I have been –
A link with only one side closed
Gripping the future
Letting go of what's past.

From me, perhaps a new part
Born to close my other side
So that I become the one
Constantly pulled.
A part of me I never knew
That from my girlhood never grew
Into one who has the need to grow
The need to change.
A part that now is as it should be
Part of you.

Mother's Message

What will you remember – some many years from now –
When I am rendered new and pure, upon a distant shore
–
What will be your feeling –
Will there be regret –
Will you sometimes miss me –
What will you forget?

Will you understand I loved you in my imperfect, human
way –
Will you know I wanted to be great every single day?
Will you recall my sense of humor –
Weird at times I know –
Goofy, silly, wha-wha, enchanting –
Peeing in my panties
Singing as I go...
Will you know I gave you all I had –
As best I could assemble
When you see the perfect Hallmark Mom –
Will I in any way resemble?

Will my faith in Jesus linger when you remember me –
Though here, I also stumbled –
Until at last, I danced free.
Free to live my calling in the cool of Autumn's days –
A new fire slowly burning –
Free from ever longing –
Released to ever praise

The one who always held me –
Even when I ran away.
The open arms still waiting.
Day by endless Day.

There needs to be a word here
Spoken from my heart.
Forgive my many failings, in time, perhaps, forget –
And know I would have stayed with you forever
When I, at last, depart.
Mother

Final Words

"Well done thou good and faithful servant"
The parable of the Talents—
These words echo through my spiritual and emotional
life.
Final Words.

I have been a people-pleaser
an approval junkie.
To the point of boredom, ridiculousness, and scandal.
Always seeking out the needy –
and the seemingly helpless –
With a burn or two to testify to my faulty judgement.

"You are a good girl – be sweet"
The final words of my mother
Before she slipped quietly away from the shores of reason
And any further words had no meaning.
Awaiting those words of approval all of my life.

Be sweet – such a Southernism –
Meaning be everything a kind and virtuous woman
Is expected to be.
Caring for others first,
giving your life away with a
big, beautiful
 well-groomed smile on your face.
Lord knows, I tried.
Looking out for others –

Spiritual coordinates noted –
Esteeming others more.

Except for one small detail –
my focus –
where I looked for approval –
the face I held up to the wrong light.
Along with all that
sweetness displayed
Violent slashes
sucker
doormat
loser-magnet.
Never enough.

"Obedience is better than sacrifice" –
so
Command me.
Turn my heart towards your will
  your way –
forever your plan –
before I was conceived.
Show me. Don't let me miss this.
Only this is enough.
And everything else is not.
Show me God what pleases you
Because anything short of you is not enough
And never will be.

"I put a pen in your hand"

A good girl, a sweet girl.
My mother's words – so healing –
restoring hope
faith in what I thought
was forever lost.
When I remember them
I am comforted –
with love
sweetest sorrow – as I truly see
she loved me always –
If a bit overly consumed with my outcomes –
Forgetting the gentle praise my heart needed.
At the end
her words gathered
all the loose and tangled threads together
shimmered deep within me like
Jesus' words.
Well Done.

I anticipate the awesome possibility.
He might speak such words over my life.
The same purge of tears
the power of love
flooding every part of me
at the thought.
Like you're a good girl
but stronger and more enduring –
Eternal.

So I take up my pen and hold it in my hand.

But Me

Fallen leaves in the melting snow
Surrounded by icy slush
I think of you...
The memory of you
Long days when no one speaks of you
Feels like melting snow.
How soon will it be not long I am thinking
When no one remembers us but me.

Zingers

It amazes me now when I see couples fight.
Did we argue like this?
To the point of real pain – exposing raw places
And pouring on all the salt.
Cold disdain shows up –
that terrible bedfellow
unwelcome guest
diehard pain –
pain that will not stop ripping up
What I ferociously call my own.

Zingers you called them.
Saying the worst out of hurt and frustration,
With breath held, waiting
For the next excuse
A chance to fight dirty right back.

I see an older couple
Helping each other on thin ice
Deceptive ice.
The kind that you can't see.
They hold each other up
Walking slow
With her hand upon his arm
His arm holding her around the waist.

I remember how we used to touch finger tips.

It was our secret language –
Our weapon when we needed
To speak softly in the middle of a crowd.
Twist up and to the right – I'm cool.
Twist down and to the left – stay close by.
No twist – get me out of here now!

If I could reach across the veil and touch you
I know how you would twist – you are cool – living large.
I am still deciding.
Some days I just long for you to be close by.
I can't lie – not to you, or to the Lord –
Sometimes I am so ready to go
ready to get out of here now.
But I am not done yet.
Save me a seat next to you?
I'll come when I'm done.

The Damage

They say it comes in waves
Well, one is washing over me
Thinking to take advantage
the element of surprise
Not that I thought I was over it
There is no over this
There is not a single day when I think that
How can the loss of one life shatter another
Strain the boundaries
beyond everything
I am learning a lesson
when I'd rather close the book
Shut it tight
No one is interested in my idle chatter
Or my daily aggravations
Hourly exclamations of living
The bill I forgot to pay
How tired I am today
The busted hose
The lawnmower that sounds as if it will soon fly to pieces
All over the yard
I want to let my pieces fly
But I fear the damage I might do....

I'm Still Here

And again today
Totally swept off my props
Away, anchors away on a river of spent emotion
Emptying what is already empty.
Until I just can't
But I do – what choice do I have
But to live in this moment until it ends.
Please, God, hold me until then.

Used up
Put away
How can an empty heart be so heavy?
I want to scream
wrestle with my fate
will myself to win this day
To pass beyond my grief, or
Find just one more hour
One routine, even tedious hour, to spend with you.
Yes, I know you are in a Better Place
A place without pain
      Without disease and death
      No sin and no disgrace
But I'm still here.
You are with God, with Abba, in Christ – so you are happy.
I am happy for you – what choice do I have
But to trust God and wait

Because I'm still here.

Lime Green

I remember the sweetness of your kisses;
We drank deeply from love's cup –
Young and innocent
astounded
weak with love.
I remember your taste
      your smell
      your touch
The way your shoulders set high and back
That distinctive walk.

That lime green washcloth
hung on the towel rack
at the back of the tub
until it was dry.
Used when you took your last shower
For our last dinner date together.
Usually, we ate at home.
I had whatever, and you had whatever you said you
wanted –
You were easy to please.

Yesterday
I held that lime green cloth to my face
Until it was no longer dry.
***Your lips drop sweetness as the honeycomb, my
bride; milk and honey are under your tongue.***
Song of Songs 4:11a

Pity Party

I could have myself
  a big old pity party
Complete with party hats
  and ice cream I should not eat.
I could cry and cry until my eyes go dry
I could turn over and just lay here in my bed for days
and into the night.
And if someone tried to be kind to me
I might say no thanks today –
Knowing they don't really want me
I'm not really welcome
My presence would only spoil the fun.
So few close friends
Less close by,
No sisters. No brothers.
No gaggle of hens to cluck inharmoniously
To my mournful song –
My dirge.
My children are on the other side of a
       whole lot of miles.

I've offered in the past
What I have not been given back
When I need it the most...
At least, it could feel that way today.
I hope tomorrow will be brighter.
Until then, I'll just stuff

all this feeling
Under my party hat and soldier on.
Pretending I'm doing fine.
I can still do that.

Snow on the Ground

In my face
Frosting my hair
Calling me back.
Calling my love to return
And embrace me as we walk
As we stop to look and share sweet kisses in the cold
O my heart!

How I yearned
For the phone to ring
Telling the news – there is snow!
My mother – silly with glee
My father – staid, somber – needing to say
That not everyone sees snow from the window
Of a warm dry house.
Aunt Carolyn, Uncle Bill hoping for more
     For snowballs
     For snowcream
     For snowmen and icicles dripping from the eaves.
Aunt Minnie announcing it is really coming down
Aunt Alma announcing it looks like it is stopping.
I remember you all.
But it is my love I want with me right now
We are separated by an invisible curtain and a little time.
My true love waits in the arms of Christ, my Savior.

I Would Marry You Again

Without skipping a beat,
But wildly, eagerly – even not knowing
What new things might blossom ....
Sooner, before – in time

We'd have babies and you would be happy
Because now I know I can talk you into anything
And make you like it.
Because that is just how much we love, you and I.

So again, and again and each time richer
(Because by now, surely, we are getting smarter)
And then again.
Even knowing, or even not knowing.
My heart knows and your heart knows

And that is enough.

All For Love

I see some things differently now.
I thought you were being stubborn when you resisted
calling the ambulance
You did that for me – so I could rest
I thought you were being selfish so many times when you
were not.
I thought you were being slick when you told me
everything
I could possibly want to hear.
When you meant every word from your heart.

I see now you were sensitive to bringing
Extra work, trouble, even worry into the house
Having long experience seeing the effects.
How you sang my praises to anyone, to everyone.
I may have wondered why...
But now I see all you did for love.
All you gave for me.

You knew how to ask for peace
When you had made war
You knew when you made a mess
And would confess --- eventually
But always willing to try
to give everything
All for love.

Recovery

One
Two become one, become family
Seek unity
harmony
Through the bump and grind
On stormy days we learn
We are one with each other and with God.
Adopted –
Reconciled –
Recovered
Full, abundant, and eternal
Access to His throne to His lap
As dear children, as family
You are home my love
In joy and comfort – asleep – waiting.
We loved.
We forgave.
We stayed true.
As we loved together, we grew.
Only to be slung against this wall of sorrow...
But the grave is defeated
Death has no sting.
I seek joy and healing.
A reason to sing.
Where is my comfort in the dark hours –
Sad and lonely hours that pass so slow
It is a mystery –

my words fall short
You are with God and so am I
Our earthly path merged
then divided
Changed in a moment
Recovery is knowing and trusting
Hope is real –
It cannot be divided.

This treasure is secure.

When We Stop to Pray

When we pause in the course of our day and
lift our hearts and minds to pray
For the sake of another, a brother, a friend –
a sister, compadre, a stranger
We put on the robe of priesthood
In the Holy Presence of Him who first loved
We are transformed by His atonement.

These days with so much in our newsfeeds,
how often do we click on sad or
post a praying set of hands or even type
I'm so sorry, Be Blessed –
but in reality, we quickly forget our compassion and
turn and leave that person with nothing more
than a Facebook reaction.

How often do we read of stinking water,
melting ice caps,
unemployment,
the ravages of disease
and instead of praying for the brokenness of mankind,
instead of praying that
redemption and restoration (the works of God) will
proclaim
His glory to all the world,
we get wordy on Facebook.

Instead of praying, we post

an angry or
sarcastic or
superior condemnation of
someone or some things.
Instead of praying, we capitulate to divisiveness
because it remains
ever easy to pluck the speck instead of
acknowledging the sin in our own hearts.

While reading my Oswald Chambers for today, I was
convicted –
as I often am when reading Oswald Chambers –
convicted, not condemned.
Conviction is a beautiful thing for it
leads out of darkness
into the light.
Conviction shows us what to do
about the darkness that is revealed in our inner being.
If you have received from His goodness
redemption and restoration,
then it is your calling to pray
for those same wonderful things to happen
always in the lives of everyone you encounter.
I acknowledge that I have not always given my utmost.

As you scroll through your Facebook feed,
allow the Holy Spirit to shine light on how
and when you should pray.

The fields are white,
it is truly harvest time, and the workers –

those priests who accept the role of intercessor –
are few.

Letter to My 40-Year-Old Self

Dear old fart.

You aren't old, but it's not the gentle breath of Spring you feel.

Maybe the warm breeze at the end of Spring and the start of Summer, which can mean perfect sunlit days (if you don't live in the South), with plenty of time to accomplish much

while you can still see what you are doing – and why.

Don't waste a minute on worry or

coulda shoulda woulda.

Sleep more and dance every time you have the chance.

Sing even if you have forgotten all the words.

Your babies are the only thing that will always give you joy.

Anything else and everyone else can be replaced if the need arises.

You can find new friends

new colleagues

new mentors

even new loves

but your babies are forever only – the beat of your heart.

You are more important than your work, no matter how important your work is.

Make time for sunsets, and lazy days.

You may have to schedule this intentionally, but once you are there, relax.

You just don't relax enough.

If there is something that burns in your heart that you want to do more than anything else – do it.

Don't wait.
Time is a thief – it steals.
You already know what I now know –
you just sometimes forget or lie to yourself.
Don't let that continue.
Embrace what you know
Trust what you believe.
You will, eventually.
Why not start sooner
and go further
and shine brighter?
Cover yourself with the unconditional love of God and
give yourself some grace.

Response From My 70-Year-Old Self

I hate to say I told you so
Even though I did
Bottom line –
Your babies are forever only
Time is a thief
Give yourself some grace.

Scripture Songs I

The Father's Song

In My house, there are many voices.

Many cultures. Many songs.

All the beauty of creation sings praises

And gives honor to the one Who was slain from the
beginning.

My full creativity and imagination are revealed

And My glory is displayed.

The earth and the heavens declare My power and majesty
--

And all the earth shouts My praise.

All of creation bows down,

But the heart of mankind is My precious jewel --

My heart's desire.

My blood and My tears poured out for love.

Everything for love.

Inspired by John 14:2

Scripture Songs II

Our Father, my father –
Abba
Papa God
You who inhabit all of the cosmos
Whose footstool is the earth –
Holy Holy Holy God
Your name is Holy.
Your kingdom –
Your rule
come now –
today.
For today is the day of my salvation.
Your will be done on earth
and in me
As it is done in all of heaven.
For You are Sovereign.
Thank you, Lord
for my daily food
which feeds the body
and for daily bread –
Rhema word which feeds my soul.
Forgive my sin, my transgression –
Every trespass against you –
Every war my pride starts –
Every rebellion in my heart.
Teach me to forgive others
in the way You forgive me.

Without pause –
Neither to weigh the cost
Nor examine the injury.
Teach me to love –
Your love in me
Poured out like a deluge
on a dry and thirsty world –
And save when temptation creeps up on me –
Deliver when evil stalks.
For the kingdom –
all authority is Yours!
All glory and goodness is Yours –
Forever and always. Amen.

Matthew 6: 9-13
In the image of the Lord's Prayer

Scripture Songs III

In Him, No Darkness

God is light – in Him, no darkness
Darkness opposes God
Darkness is doubt – fear
Bitterness (soul–rot)
Unforgiveness – prejudice
Ignorance – arrogance
Strife – greed
Lust of the flesh – the eyes – the desires of this world.
In a word – pride.
Pride of life.
What we love
Where and how we walk – embrace –
accept
Continue and prefer –
practice and repeat.
Do it your way.
Proud of what we love
Justify what we love

We ought to walk as Jesus walked.
Love as Jesus loved.
If you have anointing from the Holy One
You know all these things.
And if we sin –
and we do,

We have an advocate –
a brother –
a friend
the blood – a perfect atoning
The blood of Jesus Christ cleanses all our sins.
When we confess
When we see it –
when we acknowledge what we hear
      admit what we know
If we say we have fellowship with Him –
My Lord –
Sweet Jesus –
My God –
My King
What a friend
Lover of my soul.
If we confess Him,
yet walk – continue – practice – do –
even love and embrace Darkness –
We lie.
We do not practice the truth.
We love our darkness.

But if we walk in the light
When we pursue it – casting off ignorance, arrogance,
and strife –
When we welcome the light –
throwing out prejudice
unforgiveness –
bitterness
Like spoiled fruit –

getting the rot out of our lives
When we practice and imitate His way
When we prefer the truth over every desire –
more than anything in this world
When you would 'rather have Jesus'
Then,
We walk in the light as He is in the light.
We have fellowship with Him, and He is in us –
we are in Him
In Him, no darkness.

Inspired by: 1 John 1: 5-10

Scripture Songs VI

If you are burdened, striving for something
Rest for your soul –
His yoke is easy –
His burden is light.
Hope for the anxious heart –
ease for the troubled mind;
Come unto Jesus
gentle and kind.
Come to repentance
come uncovered
Come and find cleansing from every stain –
Find your peace in broken chains.
All includes all.
All who labor in the valley of the shadow –
Where death woos and darkness surrounds.
Suffocating on life
strangling
struggling –
Come and find rest
Take the servant's part
Partner with Him –
learn about Him
His yoke is easy –
His burden light.
Meek and lowly –
rest for my soul
Adrift in my mind –

so much to suffer
Disappointed and angry –
Yet the small voice speaks –
meek and lowly –
The still,
the lovely voice of the one
Who stands and
will not let me fall.

Matthew 11: 28-30

Scripture Songs VIII

By your loving kindness,
You have made me holy for Your glory.
You are holy and all glory is Yours –
I must clothe myself in You –
Proclaim You to all the world –
A worthy first impression –
the first thing others see –
so obvious
can't miss it.
Let me be draped like dew on the tender grass with
Your tender-hearted mercy –
Judging no one.
I am not qualified for the task – for I
cannot know what You know
see what You see –
You see what is hidden –
You know every secret of every heart.
Let me be perfectly seasoned with kindness –
So that my words and my countenance reflect Your
presence.
Let no harsh or bitter words form in my mind –
Or prostitute my lips
Nor fill the air around me with the stench of pride.
Teach me true humility and turn me away from
haughtiness –
Let me not claim superiority over anyone, for this is pride
–
Lucifer's sin.

You, O Lord, take me gently into Your arms
when I am wretched with grief
or regret.
Teach me to show that pure, gentle spirit
You have placed within me.
Let it always be, and
Flavor all my love with generous patience.
If you wait so patiently for me,
How can I stomp my foot when others are slow?
Your word tells me to make allowance for the faults of
others –
To forgive anyone that offends.
To make allowance –
leave space for the faults that will surely show –
Just as You made room for me
forgave every unholy thing –
thought and deed and neglect.
You call me to forgive others
 as you have forgiven me.
If only I could repent once
then always be found at peace
with joy
with gratitude always to my Lord, my Savior, Abba
Father
Through the power and love of the Holy Spirit which
Empowers me
comforts me
shines the light of Your holiness around me.
But I falter –
I lose my way –
sometimes I wrestle like Jacob

the clever deceiver
whom you greatly blessed before he was Israel.
Sometimes I know the way and still turn wrong.
Sometimes I don't know
but find the grace to surrender to You.
Simply trusting the One who leads me.
seeking the fullness of the Gospel –
for in You, there is all wisdom.
Teach me to embrace Your mind
so that mine will be healed.
let every word
every deed
every reaction
every move I make
Be like Christ
Think like Him
Bring peace where there is discord
Offer sweet harmony to replace the cacophonous noise.
Cleanse me of war
Make me an instrument of Your peace.

Colossians 3: 12-17

Scripture Songs X

Love is everything.
Love covers it all.
Love is greater— greatest— always first –
Better than faith and hope together –
    Even faith to move a mountain
    Even hope in things unseen
    Even more than sacrifice.
Love never fails.
If I am not wise – and, I am not, I falter –
    But if I have love in my faltering
    Instead of fear or anger –
    Or the consuming needs to be correct –
If I do not know the best way
    And stumble for the lack of light –
If I grow impatient but Love is underneath
    And draws me back –
Love will overcome my weakness.
Love is life and light. Love is wise and kind.
Love is everything good and true.
Love wins.

I Corinthians 13

Prose

For What We Can Contain

My husband and I were making plans to take cut flowers to two older friends who had recently landed in a rehab facility. I pulled out a couple of vases, one I would have liked back and was reasonably sure I could get back, and one I dubbed 'no great loss', although I have kept it for years, and would welcome it home.

Just to be sure, Rob said back to me, 'This one we expect back, and this one is a throwaway'?

As an avid gardener and flower lover, I would never throw away a vase. Horrors at the very thought!

A vase, even a plain one gleaned from a floral delivery in years past
is a valuable thing because of what it can contain--
A burst of color from the yard in the first kiss of spring
or the last breath of summer
Fruit of my planning, my planting, my sweat
my careful feeding, a constant supply of water
Or an unexpected gift from a volunteer –
Seed scattered by the wind
Our value, beloved Christian, is not in our fancy or plain
outward appearance
worth is not attributed to shiny newness
or the cloudy opaqueness that comes with great use.
We are not guaranteed anything extraordinary for our
uniqueness
or our commonness.
Our value as followers of Christ is in what we can contain

—

the Holy Spirit of our Holy Lord, Savior, Redeemer,
Friend –
the true likeness of our God who created us in His image.
God would never throw away a person.
There are no throwaway people in His eyes.
He loves each one of us simply for what we can contain.

*"Do you not know that you are a temple of God and that
the Spirit of God dwells in you?"*
I Corinthians 3:16

Heart Check

How is my heart?

I was recently challenged to consider this question.

Two scriptures were referenced as a guide to my examination.

Proverbs 4:23, read in multiple translations for the deep meaning, basically advises us to guard our heart, its desires, and affections.

What I 'take to heart',

what I hold close,

what I value and reverence,

will directly impact my journey in this precious life I have been given.

Great advice at any age, but

oh, that the younger me had grasped this truth completely.

I understood that I would reap what was sown.

I don't think I realized the degree to which I had the power to choose

what seed I scattered,

what course I followed.

I've had a few bumps in the road -- I think we all do.

The passing of years and the navigation of my course has

humbled me and taught me solid truth about the faithfulness of God.

My wandering heart has known His love and mercy –

gentle course corrections –

even rescue from the crumbling cliff.

I believe that what I love,

what I choose to honor, is critically important

to the rest of my story.

I can choose to value most, and hold closest, to my
relationship with my Heavenly Father.

The second scripture was one I've quoted many times.

Matthew 12:34 and the following verses emphasize the
eternal importance of what we speak, and how our words
testify more about our character

and what we value more than actions alone.

I confess I've used Matthew 12:34 to judge.

Additional evidence that there was a speck in another's
eye,

a broken relationship with God, because clearly

those careless, bitter words revealed a serious heart
condition.

It is easy to forget that speaking

the correct, holy-sounding words do not mean the heart
is faithful.

Likewise, it is easy to condemn someone,

even ourselves,

when the tongue starts an unintended fire.

Taken in context, and applied in conjunction with the
wisdom of Proverbs 4:23,

I am reminded to continually, daily,

in the midst of every trial,

in the midst of the longest storm, and

in the brightest moments,

always to do a heart check.

What holds my affections?

Who or what do I reverence, worship –

there is a throne at the heart of who I am.

Only God can reign there with mercy, love, and wisdom.

Only He can heal the hurt places and make me whole.

If I surrender my throne to Him,

my heart will be at peace.

And the words I speak will declare His goodness living in me.

Johnny's Country Store and Other Lost Places

Some years ago, when we still lived in Durham, my husband took me to Johnny's County Store on Roxboro Road and sent me inside to get a soda. I should have known something was up because it was not like my husband to send me inside a new place alone. Father's Day was that weekend, and I had the blues all week— I cried each time I thought about how much I longed to see my father one more time.

Even then, Johnny's was a rare place in the rapidly growing city of Durham. When it was busy you had to drive on the sidewalk to find a place to park. It is no longer there. It has been gone for a while. On that Saturday afternoon, it was busy. It was busy with children seeking treats and old men having a cold soda, catching up on the news, and talking politics. (*Folks used to talk politics without putting up a fuss, and I learned early that men gossip too.*)

I entered unaware. My husband just pulled up on the sidewalk, kindly understanding, and sent me inside. Inside to walls I had not seen in 15 years – inside to old-style drink boxes (the top slides open) – inside to hand-built wooden shelves lining the walls and the aisles. Inside to bushel baskets of local produce. Inside to a close replica of a place long gone.

'Mister J.I.' had a country store on the main drag of the small southern town where I grew up. Main drags like that have gone the way of country stores. It is getting harder to find either one; and not that many people will remember what they were like. But at Stankwytch Grocery on 2nd Street, on any given day of the week between seven in the morning and ten at night, you could find my father behind the counter – flirting with young girls, picking at young men, and sneaking candy into the hands of children. If you needed one, Mister J.I. probably had one, although it might be a little dusty. Hoop cheese, pig's feet and souse meat, johnny cakes, and RC Colas – penny candy and local produce sold by the bushel– hair tonic and lava soap. Fresh bread and honey buns. Sewing notions, watches, and Prince Albert in the can (well, let him out!). Dolls and radios at Christmas, bunnies in time for Easter, and credit if he knew you.

His customers included folks from both sides of the river, uptown and down. As a child, it seemed to me that everyone within thirty miles made time to stop there on Saturday afternoon. When it was super busy, you had to park on the street. Old men would lean against the drink box with their favorite soda and catch up on the news. And there was always news.

I did not spend much time thereafter the blue laws changed and he started selling beer. My father did not think much of his girl hanging around a place that sold beer. He slowly added packaged meat, but I remember when he smoked hams and made fresh sausage. My favorite memory is helping to bag Christmas candy – orange slices, chocolate drops, ribbon candy, chocolate-covered peanuts, and more.

As I grew up and he grew older, he would let me work at the store while he went home and rested. I only did this on the weekend because I was teaching school in Raleigh. He rested on Saturday afternoon and his faithful helper, Mr. Green, would rest on Sunday morning. This meant I missed Sunday morning church at my church in Raleigh. I was approached (only once) and told that I was back-sliding (in other words, not a good Christian) because I was working on Sunday. I replied that I had already checked in with God and I knew helping my Daddy was pleasing to God and until He told me to stop, not to look for me on Sunday morning. The truth will set you free.

Working with Mr. Green on Saturday afternoon and my Daddy on Sunday morning taught me a lot about people and a lot about myself. After he died, my mother sold the business. The new owners remodeled the old store and covered up the old walls, and parking lines were drawn.

It is hard to lose someone you love. When time had healed as much as time could, and life had gone on, it was still possible for me to find joy in memories – in a place I thought was gone forever. I found something I needed at Johnny's and the next time I need some, I think I'll let my memory walk in again, buy myself a cold RC (or the next best thing), find a place to prop, and catch up on the news.

In Loving Memory of my wonderful Father, J.I. Stankwytch

He Loves Me That Much

About my writing:

I have often felt guilt and sadness because I have accomplished so little with the gift God gave me. There are many unfinished stories, books planned but not completed, even a musical play only half done.

The Lord revealed something to me in His sweet way. I believe it is a profound truth in my life and I want to share it. It is simply this:

He does not gift us to burden us

But to make our lives full of joy.

Any expectations of what I

ought to have done

should have made time for or

whatever the snide voice of condemnation speaks over my flawed life

These are not God's expectations

His voice does not condemn me.

Those failed expectations that nip at my joy

are all my own

I have created them or willingly

picked them up along my way.

His expectations are summarized in Micah 6:8.

"He has shown you, O man, what is good,

And what does the Lord require of you?

But to do justly, and to love mercy and to walk humbly with your God."

The talent God placed in me

is not wasted because I have not met my own expectations

It is not going to be stripped away

because of my procrastination

or my bent for perfectionism.

This talent was never intended to harm me in any way

Certainly not to burden me with weighty expectations or guilt.

This gift was given freely from the heart of God for

me and others to enjoy...

but primarily for me!

He loves me that much.

When We Stop to Pray

When we pause in the course of our day and
lift our hearts and minds to pray
For the sake of another, a brother, a friend –
a sister, compadre, a stranger
We put on the robe of priesthood
In the Holy Presence of Him who first loved
We are transformed by His atonement.

These days with so much in our newsfeeds,
how often do we click on sad or
post a praying set of hands or even type
I'm so sorry, Be Blessed –
but in reality, we quickly forget our compassion and
turn and leave that person with nothing more
than a Facebook reaction.

How often do we read of stinking water,
melting ice caps,
unemployment,
the ravages of disease
and instead of praying for the brokenness of mankind,
instead of praying that
redemption and restoration (the works of God) will
proclaim
His glory to all the world,
we get wordy on Facebook.

Instead of praying, we post

an angry or
sarcastic or
superior condemnation of
someone or some things.
Instead of praying, we capitulate to divisiveness
because it remains
ever easy to pluck the speck instead of
acknowledging the sin in our own hearts.

While reading my Oswald Chambers for today, I was convicted –
as I often am when reading Oswald Chambers –
convicted, not condemned.
Conviction is a beautiful thing for it
leads out of darkness
into the light.
Conviction shows us what to do
about the darkness that is revealed in our inner being.
If you have received from His goodness
redemption and restoration,
then it is your calling to pray
for those same wonderful things to happen
always in the lives of everyone you encounter.
I acknowledge that I have not always given my utmost.

As you scroll through your Facebook feed,
allow the Holy Spirit to shine light on how
and when you should pray.

The fields are white,
it is truly harvest time, and the workers –

those priests who accept the role of intercessor – are few.

He is My Shepherd

Your correction and your protection, your step-by-step leads the way through every danger, and you comfort me. Psalm 23

There are many statements that become habitual among the people of God.

One I have noted and pondered is,

"If God brings you to it, He will bring you through it."

No doubt.

However, most every muddle I find myself in did not result from mindful following of His steps. Often, I have ignored clear direction by the Shepherd not to leave the sound of His voice, so when I feel the hook yank me back from the precipice, I cannot say He 'brought' me to it or,

'through' it. Rather, He rescued me from it.

Let's be careful in our language when we are describing the righteousness, love, and mercy of a holy God.

Yesterday, in the early morning, walking, paying little attention to roots protruding precariously in my path –

First, I saw them, and walked around them.

Then I turned around, forgot, and stumbled.

I could have been hurt.

Within just a few minutes, I repeated that.

Different roots, same near fall and result, except this time,

God reminded me that He gives angels a charge over me.

The Shepherd tried to guide me and when I would not be guided,

He rescued me.

What a picture of my life.

Does it resemble yours?

Later, He brought Psalm 23 to mind. What immediately seized my heart were the words,

'Even though I walk through the valley of the shadow of death.'

I am not sick, but remarkably healthy for my age. For that I am grateful.

But that does not mean I do not understand the landscape of that valley.

I have walked through it multiple times with people dearest to me.

I walk it now.

During my church's loud and exuberant time of praise and worship yesterday,

I sat in my chair and sobbed.

Perhaps it was a spirit of intercession,

the Holy Spirit interceding with 'groans and utterances.'

Or maybe I was just having a big old pity party.

Or maybe the gravity of walking in such a place finally grabbed my attention.

What comforted me?

His rod and his staff.

His correction and His protection.

They remind me that He is always with me, no matter what.

His eye is on this sparrow, you see.

I know He is watching.

That knowledge brings me peace, no matter what.

The Shepherd and I
Walking my path
Seeing danger, yet
filled with complacency
distracted
underwhelmed
I know Your voice but my thoughts
drown out
overcome You
Of course, I stumble
But I do not fall.
You watch over me
rescue me
correct me
guide and protect me.
Finally,
You have my attention.
For now.

A Mystery Revealed

Submission. I have struggled over the years, and, not struggled over the years (secure in absolute certainty that I understood everything). I have both fanned and ignored the tiny burning twinge that told me I might be missing something. Until the Holy Spirit opened it up to me. It was an Epiphany, a Manna Moment – it was also right there on the page in black and white English for anyone to read. How had I missed this? How had anyone? Ok, Paul. I finally hear you, brother. I do.

I am referring to "those" verses in the fifth and sixth chapter of Ephesians. You know the ones. The submit to your husband, love with the sacrificial love of Christ verses. Those verses. The ones that often give us heartburn. Because submission can be hard and so can sacrifice. I think most women understand sacrifice. I do not know what men understand, but maybe, because they try to avoid it, and fight so hard against it, maybe they understand submission.

Is Paul really speaking only to one gender at a time in this passage? I used to think so. I did not necessarily like it, but I thought I understood that Paul was speaking to a specific culture about how they ought to love and that included telling wives to submit to their husbands, children to obey their parents, and slaves to obey their masters – with a passing nod to the privileged ones who ought not to take unfair advantage of the fact that they had all of the power. But I could not accept what I have sometimes heard from pulpits. I could not accept that these verses meant anyone might be subjected to injustice or cruelty because of their inferior position in the hierarchy – that it was somehow permissible. Christ came to destroy and put to flight the hierarchies created by mankind. His yoke is easy; His burden is light.

So here I am reading it again for the umpteenth time, not

expecting much except to get past it and move on, when the Holy Spirit said wait while I shine my light on this for you. Read it again. Slowly.

Before Paul gets specific, he reminds us in verse 17 of 5 Ephesians to understand what the will of the Lord is. Ok. Let's pause right there. What is the will of the Lord? What does my Lord really want? I offer Micah 6:8 as a powerful summation. Do justice, love mercy, walk humbly. Can we do any of those things and still covet power over another? When I make it my life goal to follow these words in Micah, what room is left for me first, where is mine? Can I desire to impose my will on others? No.

Then, before I could get to the verses I usually skim over, Paul hits me with verse 21. Being submissive to one another – everyone else – in the fear of God. Before he speaks to the women of Ephesus about submission, before he speaks to husbands or children or slaves, he urges everyone who believes to be submissive to one another – in the fear of God. Remember, Paul is speaking to believers in this book, this is not an evangelistic writing, but a book full of deep truth for those who seek a closer relationship with God through his son.

It is the will of the Lord that male and female, rich and poor, every this and the other – every one of us – regardless of our position in the prevailing hierarchy – should seek to treat all others with justice, to pray and hope that all others will find mercy, and to be humble in the presence of true power, the only power that is real, the power of almighty God. **Humility is not just the opposite of pride – it is the cure.**

The Greek word Paul uses for submission in Ephesians is a military term meaning to put yourself lower in rank under another. To willingly, with humility, yield to one another in everything. I have not been delegated to a low place by God, but I am willing that God be both the exalted and the exalter. The submission that honors God is a pure heart towards others and a willingness to back down from demanding my own way. The only honor worth receiving is from God alone, and He commands me to love others as

He loves, and as I love myself. He will lift me up.

Even when my way is the right way, I need to be willing for others to see that for themselves. Even when my idea is a good one, I need to submit it humbly for examination by others. And when others claim power over me, sometimes I must let them butt their head against the love that overpowers me – and empowers me. Let them see for themselves the upside down of the kingdom that lives in me.

From the Message: Philippians 2:3

Don't push your way to the front; don't sweet talk your way to the top. Put yourself aside; and help others get ahead.

Down is the new up!

On Eagles Wings

Isaiah 40:31 They that wait upon the Lord will renew their strength, they will mount up on wings like eagles; they will run and not grow weary, they will walk and not faint.

Whenever I hear the words from this line of scripture in Isaiah, I immediately flashback to 1976. That awful hot summer following the spring of my great shame. My college graduation had passed me by, left me hanging my head and avoiding parental encounters. That graduation that should have happened – with friends and classmates – the one my parents had eagerly anticipated – that one – derailed for the lack of one required course. My last college credit required for graduation was a physical education course. That's right, PE.

How could this happen, you ask? How could a smart girl with parental support and expectations let this happen? Ah. I had failed horseback riding – because they put me on a horse the size of Nevada. I had to use a stepladder to mount this beast. He was part Clydesdale and full of vinegar – at least he was my excuse when I stopped going to class. Then, not going to badminton for who knows why (I loved it and was half decent at the game); missing tennis class until I was ashamed to go back; passing golf by the skin of a hole-in-one – only accepted by the instructor because I had several amazed witnesses. I also failed archery (I could not pull the bow) and croquet (can't remember why) – you get the picture. Not going and then not knowing how to fix not going became my M.O. for not passing yet another PE course.

When I did not graduate with my class, I had to move off campus into a tiny, dingy, buggy little place that was damp and bothered my breathing. I was waitressing at night in a seafood restaurant carrying trays that were bigger than me and lining hot plates along my arm. Not exactly a great time in my life except for one thing. I had briefly tried a job driving an ice cream truck – which I bounced off the back of a tractor-trailer (another story for another time). While driving this truck, I had started singing because I could not hear the radio over the roar. The songs I knew the best were hymns of the church. Through the old tried and true messages of "Near the Cross", "Great is Thy Faithfulness" and "Softly and Tenderly" (to name a few), I reclaimed my faith in Christ and began going back to church. It was in a tiny Foursquare Church in Raleigh that I learned the chorus that would soon play a role in pulling my fanny out of the fire.

In unrealistic expectation of getting 'in shape', I thought I would be motivated to rise early (7 AM) (after waitressing late) and willingly subject my chubby self to rigorous physical conditioning – in the heat and humidity of NC in the summertime. I wanted the result, I wanted the fantasy, but I was not prepared for the sacrifice. I should have taken a course that came with air conditioning, like ping pong or darts.

Because I was not conditioned or committed, and a little depressed, I hated the very thoughts of this class – the getting up too early – making the long trek from the parking lot – the sweating profusely and the gasping and grunting – all in front of cute girls in cute shorts and t's who were already more in shape than I had any hope of becoming. I was overweight, out of shape, and discouraged. And my only cute shorts had gotten too tight since last summer.

Because of all of this, I forgot to go. I made excuses and lofty resolutions. I went and turned around and slinked away – in short, I skipped this class over and over. Talk about missing the mark – if that is the definition of SIN, I was headed for trouble deep and as the end of the summer class approached, I knew I was about to be found out. Insert my Daddy's voice in my head – *Rosemary, be sure your sin will find you out* – I was going to fail conditioning and that meant I was going to fail to graduate for the SECOND time!

I did not know how to fix this, and the stress would not let me have a moment's peace. I finally confided in a friend from church, and she convinced me to go speak with the instructor and ask for a way out – to literally throw myself at her mercy. I think the instructor was truly staggered by my request – that anyone would make such a ridiculous request when I had not shown up for class. But she did offer me a way out – I believe she was utterly convinced that I would fail and so, failure might make a great object lesson for future wayward conditioners. She told me if I could pass the final "exam", she would pass me for the course and I could graduate.

On the morning of the "exam", I got up on time and walked into that gymnasium, ready I thought to pass whatever was thrown at me. Because I knew how to take a test. I was just as chubby and unconditioned as ever, but I was determined. Because I just had to do this.

"This" was a million or so laps around the gym, to be completed in a prescribed amount of time. I could walk for a break but could not stop moving and had to finish on time. So, I ran, and walked, and ran, and ran some more – I had to keep moving – and so I did. It was brutal.

With about 25% of the million left to go, I stopped having the occasional stab in the side that I could walk off and broke into a continuous, unrelenting pain on both sides that absolutely stole my breath. I could feel the wall I was about to hit. Walking did not help. As I dragged one foot after the other and clutched my sides, the Lord dropped a command directly into my mind.

Sing that chorus – they shall run and not grow weary; they will walk and not faint – raise your hands high above your head in praise and run.

Either too stunned or too desperate to argue – I obeyed. Immediately. No questioning – is that really you, God? No doctrinal egg-flipping – just ok. And immediately, the pain eased, then stopped completely. I ran with arms flapping on high – slowly, steadily, and no longer thinking I was going to die – with only one thing in my mind and that was God's Word through a song. More importantly, this chorus became His right now word to me in my right now moment of need. I sang loudly enough to be heard and

I really began to praise Him as it got down into my soul what He was doing for me. I sang and praised, and I made it to the end of the course!

When I had finished the entire million on time (just), the instructor motioned me over to the record table and she looked at me with the strangest look. Confused, maybe a little annoyed. I'm not sure how to describe it. Then, a quirky, half-smile, half-smirk, "I didn't think you could do this. I absolutely knew you could not." Pregnant pause, "Who told you to do that?"

"Do what?" I wheezed.

"Lift your hands above your head."

Still too amazed to prevaricate, "God?" I replied as a gasp.

"Explain yourself. Now."

Ummm – "God told me to sing and praise Him and to lift my hands above my head."

She explained that this is a runner's trick. When you run, your lungs expand. As they expand, they press against the ribs, and this is what causes that stabbing pain in the side. She saw me struggling with that pain. When I lifted my arms, I also lifted my rib cage – allowing my lungs to expand at the bottom.

Finally, she shook her head and uttered the most precious verdict – "Ok. You pass."

As I turned to go, I realized there were stragglers behind me who appeared to be 'in shape' bent over with their hands on their knees.

I raised mine and lived.

I gained a prize I had not earned because I obeyed the Lord.

An Empty Chair at the Table – A Thanksgiving Day Devotion

I googled Thanksgiving...
the first three things that popped up were
food, football, and movies! Ok...

Then I googled Thanksgiving's purpose...
"a public celebration in acknowledgment of
divine favor or kindness
a day set apart for giving thanks to God."
I like that.

But sometimes, things have happened
or failed to happen in such a way that
our thanksgiving
maybe a little broken, a little dismayed.
We all know of someone who is dealing with
the first Thanksgiving
without someone precious.
Maybe you will be looking at an empty chair –
missing that one dear face
that made every occasion richer, more blessed.
This year, we are looking forward to sharing our meal
with
true friends that live in our neighborhood.
We will use the big dining room table
and candles
and good dishes
because that is part of our tradition.

But I would be lying if I denied

I would rather be anywhere with my children and grandchildren.

Remember, in the Bible, (I Thessalonians 5: 16-18) we are encouraged to give thanks in all circumstances, but, in our human weakness, that can often feel hard to do.

While I was googling – I ran across an essay written by an American-Asian woman entitled "Rice for Thanksgiving".

She wrote about how the cultures combined at her grandma's table

with mounds of steamed white rice (the Asian way)

and plenty of rich brown, American gravy.

I also read about the empty chair tradition of the Jewish people –

called Elijah's chair –

part of their Passover meal tradition.

That got me thinking about that extra chair,

that extra place at the table.

A contemporary Jewish writer explained the relevance of Elijah's chair

(and sometimes, Elijah's cup) this way:

"Until injustice, violence and greed disappear, we remain enslaved.

Until God makes his home on earth, we have not truly left Egypt."

An experience that I have been blessed to be part of over the past 15 years is the

Walk to Emmaus retreat.

One of my favorite things is the singing of the meal blessing –
out of this,
a new tradition was born for me.
When I say grace now,
I always invite Jesus to join me at the table.

Gathered at this table, Holy Spirit come
Fill us with your presence, bind our hearts as one.
Bless this time together, Jesus, give us peace
Come, Lord, be with us, join us as we meet.
Come, Lord, be with us. Bless this food we eat.

I have also been thinking a lot about Thanksgiving feasts
when I was a child.
Lord, my mother really threw it down!
She had so much variety –just a taste of everything would yield
two big plates
heaping full
and running over.
I have tried to replicate that in the past,
but no more.
I have learned you do not have to eat the memory to appreciate it.

Is there an extra chair at your table this year?
Come, Lord, be part of our memories,
part of our conversation,
join in our fellowship with friends, with family –
and bless us with your sweet presence
whether we are feasting with a multitude,

or seated quietly alone.
Come, God, make your home in me.
Fill me with your presence and set my spirit free.

Matthew 25:35-40.

When we offer a chair to the outcast,
to the orphan,
to the poor,
to the forgotten,
we extend a chair
to the Lord who loves us all.

Myrtle Ruth's Thanksgiving Menu
Biscuits, rolls, and fried cornbread.
Rice and gravy, stewed beef, and corn dumplings.
Fried chicken,
chicken and pastry
(not dumplings,
but strips of rich, egg dough,
cut in strips, and hung up to dry)
'dressing' made with chopped chicken and cornbread and
white bread and onions...
Served with canned, jellied cranberry sauce *a complete
meal and feast right by itself!*
Turnips and collards,
green beans and squash casserole,
fried squash, fried okra.
Field peas with steamed okra pods on top, almost black
with pepper
Mashed potatoes, potato salad, new potatoes.
Fried fat back, green lima beans, brown butterbeans.

Corn on the cob and creamed corn.
And the centerpiece was not a turkey,
it was a big old juicy ham with candied fruit.
Oh, and a fruit salad and deviled eggs.

And Lord don't even get me started on dessert.
Well, ok.
Sweet potato pie, coconut pie, pecan pie,
pound cake, red velvet cake,
and pineapple (upside down)
22 layer chocolate cake (not a typo – 22).
Sweet tea that could stand up by itself.
And coffee with dessert.
Homemade lemonade for the young at heart.

Happy Thanksgiving Ya'll!!

To My Daddy's Family on Thanksgiving Day 1998

Today, I thank God for this family
In-laws and out-laws; uncles and aunts;
Three generations of Grandmas,
Cousins to fourth or fifth at last count.

I wish every family had what ours has,
As we give Thanks to our maker above;
Recalling the old days to laugh or to cry for;
Adding today to the treasures stored.

Each year my desire to come deepens;
While the pressure to do otherwise swells.
I miss all who have "gone on" before us,
And the ones who don't come anymore.

Heavy Heavy Heavy Laid Down

Heavy heavy heavy laid down
For a long time carried
For a long time buried
For long endless days my master.
Deep crusted heart made tender
Made new
I am tender, I am free
Horse and rider thrown into the sea.

Lyrics

Saving My Tears

You alone are with me when I feel so all alone
You know all about the state I'm in
You alone can comfort me
You alone can save
Beneath your wings, I find the rest I need.
I often am distracted by the roaring of the waves –
As the storm you have allowed me rages on.
I become afraid when I turn my eyes away
From the glory and the power of your love.
But you keep giving me grace
Bringing me hope
Turning the darkness into light.
Taking my fear
Taking my shame
Saving my tears. Saving my tears.

It seems I've always known you.
Even as I struggle on –
To see and know the wonder that is you.
You alone can see my heart.
Only you can love me still
Your kindness chases all my fears away.
You are giving me grace
Bringing me hope
Turning the darkness into light.
Taking my fear
Taking my shame

Saving my tears. Saving my tears. Saving my tears.

In the Arms of Jesus

He named me, He framed me
He calls me every hour
He loves me, He saves me
He fills me with His power.
In the eyes of the world,
I'm not much to admire –
But in the arms of Jesus
In the arms of Jesus
In the arms of my sweet lord,
My heart is set on fire.

He's with me, I feel Him
His tender love and grace
And one day soon I'll see Him
I'll look upon that face.
Though in the eyes of the world
He's not much to admire—
In the eyes of His bride
Yes, in the eyes of His bride
In the eyes of His bride
He sets our hearts on fire.

I can not find the words to tell
Just what he's done for me
But I am His, bought with a price
Bound for eternity.
Our bridegroom comes in glory

To take us to His side
And when we reach that golden shore
Oh when we reach that golden shore
At last, upon that golden shore
We will be satisfied.

In the arms of Jesus
Wrapped in the arms of Jesus
Forevermore with Jesus
We will be satisfied.

Power

I went to the ocean
Just to walk upon the sand
The tide rolled in before me
And I felt His mighty hand.
I sang songs of praise to Him
As the waves came crashing in
I sang praises to the one
Who washed away my sin.

I went to the garden
Just to smell the sweet perfume
Early in the morning
When the Rose of Sharon blooms
I sang songs of praise to Him
As the day came crashing in
I sang praises to the one
Who washed away my sin.

I danced in the evening
And in the morning light
I danced for my creator
And felt His pure delight.
I sang songs of praise to Him
And in that precious hour
He heard my songs of praise to Him
And He filled me with His power

Power, power
There is life-changing power
In the cleansing blood of the Lamb.
Power, power
There is wonder-working power
In the precious blood
Of God's perfect Lamb.

lyrics

God, You Are the Bomb

Can you hear me now?
Can you hear me now?
Can you hear me now?

In this world of cell phones and technology
I'm searching for a plan that brings you close to me
Your endless love is always online
Your minutes don't expire – your plan is divine.

God, you are the bomb – dot com
With a high-speed connection
Your spirit searches my heart – my heart
And you give the best directions

When I search for Truth, the Bible is my guide.
When I search for Peace, you're always on my side.

God, you are the bomb – dot com
With a high speed connection
Your spirit searches my heart – my heart
And you give the best directions

I hear you now
I hear you now
I hear you now

Communion Song

We must be broken like bread on the altar
We must be poured out like wine.
Jesus has called us to be as His brothers
And share in His sacrifice.

Lord, you were broken like bread on the altar
Your cleansing blood spilled like wine
You paid our ransom and in this communion
We honor Your sacrifice.

As individuals and as a community of faith, we are being
broken. And that's ok because we know Who is pruning
us and that He knows how to produce His harvest.

Just as essential as the breaking, is what we pour out.
Now is the time to pour out contention, doubt, and fear
on the altar of His grace. Let Him replace all of that
with His love, peace, and joy and teach us to love each
other as He has loved us. His perfect, unconditional,
sacrificial love. The peace that comes when we honestly
seek His will. The joy of our salvation.

And together as a community of faith and the body of
Christ, in one accord, seek the face of the Author and
Finisher of our faith. Seek to serve our Risen Lord. Hope
to share in His harvest.

Oh God You Are My God (Psalm 63)

I thirst for you; I long for you;
I search for your hand.
For it seems I've lost my way
And my heart has gone astray – again.
In my darkest night, I remember you.
In this dry and weary land –
Where nothing lovely grows,
And no living waters flow –
I need my friend.

Oh God, you are my God –
How could I forget –
The power of your tender loving hand?
Without you, I must fall,
But with you, I will stand.
Oh God, you are my God.

Now I cling to you;
For I have tried
To live my life apart
From the shelter of your heart –
It did not satisfy.
Lord, I want to stay
In that holy place
Where your glory and your power
Are with me every hour –
Life is better there.

Oh God, you are my God –
I will not forget –
The power of your tender loving hand.
Without you, I must fall,
But with you, I will stand.
Oh God, you are my God.

Oh God, you are my God –
I lift up my hands.
With all my heart I praise your name.
Without you, I must fall,
But with you, I will stand.
Oh God, you are my God.

For Libby

Waterfall

Day and night, life moves too fast
And rocks are in the way
I try to find a place at last
Where I can be okay
I see the wonders of Your hand
The rocks and trees cry out
I am a child who wants to know
What love is all about?

It feels like a waterfall –
Your love flows over me
Love like a waterfall
I really need to be
Washed in the waterfall.

I have wandered like this stream
Searching for a pool
Looking for a different dream
Breaking every rule
Hoping trusting knowing You –
What I'm finding now
The way the truth the life in You –
This time I'm learning how
To dance in the waterfall

I sing in the waterfall
Your love pours over me

You sound like a waterfall
Alive inside of me.

It feels like a waterfall –
Your love flows over me
Love just like a waterfall
I really need to be
Washed in the waterfall.

I listen to the waterfall.
Washed in the waterfall.
Clean in the waterfall.

Psalm 42: 7

Caught in the Overflow

Caught up in sorrows, covered in shame
Worn by the struggle, alone and afraid
Broken and burdened, condemned to the night –
But God sent His Word – Speaking life – speaking light.
Caught in the overflow – declaring good news
In power and glory, I am renewed.

Caught by His goodness, joy fills my cup
Restored by His power, cleansed by His love
Kinsman Redeemer – Breaking My Chains
With power and glory, in His holy name.
Caught in the overflow – all that remains –
Is power and promise, in His precious name.

Caught in the overflow, blessings flow free
God's Holy Spirit, living in me.
No stain remains, no longer a slave
Fully adopted, delivered I stand –
Free in His presence, carved in His hand.

Come Holy Spirit, fill up my heart
Break every chain that keeps us apart
Show me your glory here in this place
Flood me with mercy, abundance, and grace.
Show me your glory, right where I stand
Cover my weakness with your loving hand.

Your hiding place is high and secure.
Reveal your glory – make my heart pure.

Draw Me Nearer

Draw me just a little bit closer
I want to be like you.
Scrub my cup on the inside, Lord
Make my heart brand new.

Draw me just a little bit closer
Keep my hand on the plow.
I want to work in your vineyard,
The fields are ready right now!

Draw me just a little bit closer,
Down on my knees, I must fall.
I've been feeling the spirit.
I've been hearing the call.

Draw me just a little bit closer,
Changed by your glorious grace.
Create me again in your image.
So I can look in your face.

Just a closer walk with thee
Grant it Jesus, this my plea –
Daily walking close to thee
Let it be, dear Lord, let it be.
Draw me nearer, nearer blessed Lord,
To the cross where thou hast died.
Draw me nearer, nearer, nearer blessed Lord –

To thy precious, bleeding side.

The Victory Song

I've got a victory coming over me
And now, the mountain top I see
I've been climbing steadily
And now I feel a victory coming.

If you feel defeated,
And tempted thus to sin
Remember Jesus promised
His strength is greater than
Even on your worst day
When you think you can't win --
You're still more victorious than
The enemy's ever been!

You've got a victory coming over you
That mountain top is still in view!
Just keep climbing till you're through
And then you'll have a victory coming on.

Jesus loves the sinner,
Of that, I have no doubt.
I was locked up in my sin
But Jesus let me out!
He heals the broken-hearted
And sets the captive free!
He'll win the battle for you –
And give you victory!

You'll have a victory coming over you
That mountaintop is shining through
Trust in God and when you do
You'll know you have a victory coming on.

Amazing Love

There's a lot to be said for the sweet love of God
Our minds can not comprehend
All that He is and all that He did
And all that He has in store.
His precious heart suffered and cried
And bled on Calvary's tree.
He gave His all that I might live,
He died to make me His.

Amazing love! Amazing love!
He loved me even then.
Scorned and ashamed
He shouldered the blame
And loved away my sin.

There is a God in Zion's Hill –
His mighty arm is mighty still!
All nature moves at His command
And every life is in His hand.
And soon, He'll tell King Jesus
To come again and reign.
And save this lovely world of His
From all its death and pain.

Amazing love! Amazing love!
He loved me even then.
Broken and sore,

He settled the score
And loved away my sin.

Only what's lovely, good, and true
When Heaven comes down
And everything's new.
The lamb will be praised
And the bride will be raised
His love, her only crown

Amazing love! Amazing love!
He loves us all the same.
Behold the one who takes away
All our guilty stain.

Amazing love! Amazing love!
He loves the broken heart.
Believe that He lives and take what He gives ---
A love that will not fail.

See Him

I will sing a new song
I will praise Him all day long
I want the world to see my Lord.
See Him in His beauty
See in His grace
See the tender love upon His face

See Him in the manger.
See Him on the cross
See Him as the answer
When they think all is lost.
See His act of mercy
For those He came to save
See Him in His splendor
Risen from the grave.

See Him never-ending
See Him still the same
See Him as their savior
And call upon His name.

Bread of Heaven

Come and taste the Bread of Heaven
Breathe in the Living Word
Drink deeply of that water
It quenches every thirst
There's a voice gently pleading
Just to make your heart His throne
God is with us
God is faithful
He will not leave you alone.

He's my friend when friends forsake me
He provides my every need
King of Heaven, my companion
I must follow where You lead.
Jesus is the bread of Heaven
He is the Holy Word.
Every eye will see His glory
Every tongue proclaims His worth.
All praise to the Lord of the earth
All praise to the Lord of the earth

Sweet Jesus

I am only here because
your love
I am only here because
        your grace and mercy
Even in
My darkest hour
you are there
And by your power
I am standing here
to sing your praise, Jesus

Jesus, oh Jesus
You are every story that I love
Oh Jesus
You are every song I have
Every moment that I savor
You are every glory from above
Sweet Jesus

When I think of all I've done
All the places I've run
Broken forgotten days
Every blessing
Every praise
Still, you're standing in my place
Dying, pouring out
your grace

My sweet Jesus.

Jesus, oh Jesus
You are every story that I love
Oh Jesus
You are every song I have
Every moment that I savor
You are every glory from above
Sweet Jesus

You are every song I have
Every moment that I savor
You are every glory from above
Sweet Jesus

Just Like Before

Falling in love again, Singing with joy again
Living for Jesus -- Just like before.
Finding my way again
Finding that peace again
Finding forgiveness -- Just like before.

In doubt, I turned away and I lost everything --
Then He called my name -- Just once more.
His kindness saw my need, His mercy heard me plead
And now, It's just like before.

Falling in love again
Singing with joy again
Living for Jesus
Just like before.
Knowing I'm born again
Knowing His heart again
Filled with His spirit
Just like before.

His kindness saw my need
His mercy heard me plead
And now
It's just like before.

One Touch

One touch from the nailed scarred hand
One touch from God my creator
And everything old is made new
Everything cold is made over.

One touch from His wounded side
And all of my fears try to hide
But they're brought to the light
For the dark is made bright
In the light of His precious love.

Rosemary Stankwytch Long

"What little can be said about me counts little except for this – To live is Christ."

Rosemary Stankwytch Long has been a writer almost her entire life. Over the years, she has denied her poetic muse and settled for the much unacclaimed but needed 'tool shed' that Thoreau wrote about – literally working as a technical writer for much of her public career. At the center of everything she writes now is her dedication to life in Christ. Through the power of the Holy Spirit working in her life, she aspires to become someone who puts Christlikeness on display in her life and writing. Rosemary was born in Lumberton, North Carolina, and married the love of her life in 1990. High school sweethearts, Robert and Rosemary were married for 32 years; they loved each other for 52 years.

She is happiest in the company of her "babies" both new and old. They include biological daughters Ruth and Beth, 'adopted' daughter Brittany; and grandchildren John, Eleanor, Wyatt, and Wesley – in birth order. Add to that Nacho from Madrid and the children of her friends. She has two very best friends: one from kindergarten and one from college days. Rosemary graduated from Meredith College in 1976. She is also best friends with a short and sassy toy poodle/terrier rescue named Mikey. And yes, Mikey loves everybody!

www.ingramcontent.com/pod-product-compliance
Lightning Source LLC
Chambersburg PA
CBHW031503120626
46545CB00005B/1725